DE MO

J AE

Please re n this b on ate mped

THE
FUTURE FOR
WOODLAND
DEER

THE FUTURE FOR WOODLAND DEER

MANAGEMENT OR SPORT?

Roger McKinley

SWAN·HILL
PRESS

First published in the UK in 1999
by Swan Hill Press, an imprint of Airlife Publishing Ltd

British Library Cataloguing-in-Publication Data
A catalogue record for this book
is available from the British Library

ISBN 1 85310 973 8

The following abbreviations denote the photographer and will be found at the end of each photo caption within this book.

RM Roger McKinley.
VP Victor R. Pardy, Forest Enterprise Leading Ranger, Ringwood Forest.
SV Stuart Venables, Deer Manager, Dorset.
RT Robert Thurlow, Forest Enterprise Leading Ranger, Sussex.

Typeset by Servis Filmsetting Ltd, Manchester
Printed in England by Butler & Tanner Ltd, Frome and London

Swan Hill Press
an imprint of Airlife Publishing Ltd
101 Longden Road, Shrewsbury, SY3 9EB, England
E-mail: airlife@airlifebooks.com
Website: www.airlifebooks.com

To Pat and Avril,

two long-suffering wives, who have borne Alan's and my long
absences, unsocial hours and the family pressures inherent in
managing deer without complaint, and with great support, over all
of these long years.

Also

in memory of my dear mother and father, whose support never waned,
and whose love was unconditional.

ACKNOWLEDGEMENTS

In putting this book together I have been helped by many of the people that you will meet throughout the text, and I owe them all a debt of gratitude. My main roles seem to be those of scribe and catalyst; I bring people together, exchange ideas and gather information, then put the whole thing together as a package. But I depend upon friends and colleagues to help develop ideas and bring them to fruition, and to question and challenge throughout the process. Usually the best practitioners are those who do a hard, often difficult job day after day, but are not able to devote the time to writing about it. I have learned from them all, and this is my way of thanking them and giving something back. I am truly grateful that they trust me enough to allow me to write about them.

It would be impossible to thank everybody who has helped me during those years, but there are some whom I must pick out for a special mention.

Fred Courtier, formerly Head Forester, Wildlife, with the Forestry Commission, who assessed my 1967 Forestry School project on fallow deer, which won first prize that year, and which started me on a path which I still tread to this day.

The officers and members of the old Teign Valley Deer Management Society (1978–86) and in particular Fountain Forestry Ltd, all of whom helped and encouraged me in my early tentative efforts to implement my ideas of management within a wild population of fallow deer.

Jack and the late Pam Yeatman, Austin and Jo Yeatman and Helen and the late Brian Young, Dorset landowners for whom Alan Lewis and I have managed deer for the last seventeen years. They have trusted, helped and encouraged us, whilst letting us try different ideas free from interference. I hope that they will realise their immense contribution, without which this book would never have seen the light of day, and accept my most grateful thanks. Brian Young's unexpected death after the book had been delivered to the publishers has meant that I can only acknowledge his contribution posthumously to his family, and not to Brian personally, as I would have wished.

English China Clays Ltd, who entered into an agreement in 1984 with Alan and me, and later with Stuart Venables, to manage deer on some of their lands in the Purbecks, an agreement which, with very little modification, has stood to this day.

The late Tony Burrey, a good and dear friend who played a vital part by reading the text for me, and commenting on the way in which it came over to a 'typical' reader. This required an ability to 'nit-pick', in itself an uncomfortable exercise, but one which has, in my view, led to many subtle improvements. Tragically Tony also died very suddenly whilst the text was with the publishers, so again I shall only be able to acknowledge his contribution posthumously. I am deeply indebted to Tony, for the dedicated way in which he approached this rather thankless task.

Derek Stocker, Forest Enterprise Chief Ranger (retired 1998), for much help, information and advice during the preparation of the book.

Keith (Brad) Bradbury, Forest Enterprise Chief Ranger, for allowing me to tap into his vast store of knowledge about the habits and management of muntjac in woodland habitats.

Jane Karthaus, the Association of Professional Foresters, for providing up-to-date information on typical costs of tree shelters and deer fencing.

Airlife Publishing (Swan Hill Press) for taking a chance both with an unknown author and also a controversial slant to a familiar subject; and also for a number of subtle improvements in respect of text organisation.

I am also indebted to the following for permission to use quotations from published works:

The British Association for Shooting and Conservation (BASC), for permission to use facts and figures from their 1997 Deer Stalking Survey.

Shooting Times, Country Magazine and Mr Dominic Griffith, professional stalker, for permission to use quotations from articles in those publications.

Forestry and British Timber for permission to use quotations from an article published in that publication.

Mr Roger Buss, professional hunting guide for permission to quote material from published articles.

Mr Richard Prior, deer consultant and author of many books about deer, for permission to use his description of required shooting standards from *Roe Stalking*, in the '*Shooting Times* Library' series.

Laurence Pollinger Ltd and the estate of the late Ralph Wightman, for permission to use quotations from *Portrait of Dorset* and *Abiding Things*.

Mr E.T.C. Bourke and Mr C. Sturge for respectively sourcing and giving me permission to use the quotation from *A History of Ashmore* which features in Chapter 3.

Stanley Paul, the publishers of *Shooting and Stalking*, edited by Charles Coles, for permission to use quotations by P.C. Baillie and the late Lt-Col R.H.A. (Jock) Cockburn.

New Forest District Council, for permission to use material from their leaflet about Lyme disease.

I would also like to offer my heartfelt thanks to Forest Enterprise (South and West England), and in particular Rod Leslie (Acting Regional Director 1997–8), Tim Sawyer (Regional Operations Manager 1997–8) and Oliver Lucas (Forest District Manager, Dorset 1997–8), both for their permission to describe the work carried out by Dorset Forest District staff, and for their help and encouragement over the years. Tim Sawyer has allowed me to use some of his observations about deer management, which have been gathered from various South and West (England) internal papers, and I thank Oliver Lucas for his contribution to the spreadsheet section. Rod Leslie kindly contributed the foreword, for which I am especially grateful.

Finally, responsibility for the accuracy of the text remains mine alone. I hope that there are not too many errors, although there may be many differences of opinion. All photographs were taken by me unless otherwise credited. My grateful thanks are due to Vic Pardy (Forest Enterprise Leading Ranger in Dorset), Robert Thurlow (Forest Enterprise Leading Ranger in Surrey), Stuart Venables (self-employed deer manager based in Dorset), Derek Stocker (Forest Enterprise Chief Ranger) and my son Jeremy McKinley for their photographic contributions.

Author's note:

A short while after I left school I joined the Forestry Commission, the government forest service. In the early 1990s this organisation was reorganised into two distinct parts, still under its overall umbrella. Forest Enterprise (FE) is the agency which manages the woodlands owned by the nation, whilst the Forestry Authority (FA) is responsible for plant health, tree-felling controls, grant-in-aid and legislative functions. All three names will appear throughout the text, depending upon which applied at the time when the event being described occurred.

South and West England is the name given, at the time of writing (1997) to the region which, in broad terms includes all Forest Enterprise land south and west of a line from Liverpool to London.

Several FE staff have retired or changed jobs or grades since the text was completed. Any grades or jobs described herein, refer to those applying at the time of writing (1997).

FOREWORD

The increase in range and numbers of deer in lowland England is one of the most extraordinary changes in our wildlife this century. It has taken place so quietly that only now are many people realising quite what is happening. Today I rarely visit a Forestry Commission wood without seeing deer, and more often than not spot two or three roe bounding over open countryside in Wiltshire when travelling in the London train.

With deer come benefits and problems, and the biggest problem by far is that they simply don't fit into the traditional management of the lowlands. So when they make their presence felt by eating trees or roses, solutions can be hard to find. Keepers don't welcome rifle fire during the pheasant season and effective deer management without neighbourly co-operation can be hard to achieve. But it can be done – and Roger McKinley's book addresses the issues head on, backed by a wealth of practical experience from his many years of deer management in southern England.

What is the difference between stalking and deer management? Need there really be a conflict between pheasants and deer management? What equipment and training do you need to manage deer? It's all here in this book, and slips down easily with a mixture of personal experience and reminiscences of the many eminent deer-men Roger has worked with.

Roger's love of deer shines through every page – and here is the most important lesson of all, that without natural predators, we as land managers have a duty to look after deer. That often means preventing their population growing too high for land and for the deer themselves. But that does not mean hating deer, or wanting to exterminate them – exactly the opposite: with more and better management we can share the countryside with deer and enjoy seeing these beautiful creatures as part of the daily scene.

This is a book for anyone who wants to stalk deer and for land managers of all sorts. As manager of 250,000 acres of Forestry Commission woodland, I am acutely conscious of the need for more and better deer management in the English lowlands. Please read this book, it will be an eye opener.

Rod Leslie
Regional Director,
Forest Enterprise,
South & West England.

CONTENTS

INTRODUCTION

My reasons for writing this book

During the course of my occupation as a professional forester and woodland manager I meet many people – landowners, foresters, conservationists and farmers in particular – who are suffering damage from deer, usually to woodlands. Many people complain, legitimately in my view, that deer control does not work, or is failing to meet their needs.

I have heard such complaints many times over many years, yet I know from my own experience that things can be different. Having worked for the Forestry Commission for thirty-two years (during which time I was involved in, or professionally responsible for, deer management in various forests) and having also undertaken deer management on a number of private estates of varying sizes, I believe that it is quite possible to manage fallow, sika and roe deer so that damage to woodlands, farm crops and conservation sites is minimised, and I have little doubt that the same is true of red deer. Muntjac present a totally different set of problems whilst Chinese water deer rarely seem to be in need of close control because of their limited distribution, and few stalkers (only the lucky ones) will get the chance to work with them. One thing is certain however: in order to achieve these woodland management objectives, it is necessary to change our approach towards deer work.

Where deer live in woodlands whose long-term health and vitality is important, there is a real need to move away from regarding them as a sporting resource, and to see them instead as an integral part of woodland management. Then the management of deer can be structured so that whatever objectives are seen as necessary for woodland viability (and, incidentally, deer as well) can be achieved. In other words priorities should be arranged so that the objectives of any chosen deer management system are dictated by the needs of woodland management rather than dealt with as a separate and primarily sporting issue, as is commonly the case at present. It is possible, in my opinion, to accommodate recreational hunting as part of successful deer management in managed woodlands, but only if the requirements of the chosen woodland management system are given precedence. In this way recreational

> **Whilst deer stalking is a sister sport to game shooting and wildfowling, it stands rather separate; not only because of the larger size of the quarry but also because the weapon used is the rifle and not the shotgun.**
>
> **P.C. Baillie, from *Shooting and Stalking*, edited by Charles Coles.**

Recreational hunting as part of a planned deer management system. (RM)

hunting forms one part of a deer management system and the deer management system forms part of a woodland management system. When affairs are ordered in this way there is little confusion about priorities.

It is my hope that the experiences which have contributed to the production of this book may provide some ideas and useful ways forward for readers who are facing the challenge of integrating woodland and deer management, especially where strong conflicts and problems have been identified and where a need for different solutions has been recognised.

Although I will argue deer numbers often need to be substantially reduced, I do not do so in an uncaring sense – in fact quite the contrary. Like most foresters I recognise that if Britain wants managed woodlands or commercial forests to be viable – and it matters not whether they are being managed for timber production, game shooting, conservation, coppicing or simply the landowner's enjoyment – it will be necessary either to contain deer numbers at artificially low levels, or to accept the potentially high costs of protection measures. In those instances where woodland viability has been achieved without expensive tree protection, both woodlands and deer remain

Healthy woodlands in spite of deer. (RM)

healthy, and although this is achieved using 'artificial' methods, that should not be a cause for concern since in our small, heavily populated island, virtually all land management (even for conservation) is, by necessity, artificial to a greater or lesser degree. This will be my starting point, and the book is targeted particularly at deer management in the woodlands and habitats of lowland England.

The people who feature in this book

During my career I have had the privilege of knowing, and often working with, many full-time professional stalkers, some of whom work for the Forestry Commission, while others are employed by individual estates and still others are self-employed and work for different landholdings. I also know many part-time stalkers who stalk for deer management groups or private landowners. Some have become valued friends, indeed my closest friend, Alan Lewis, became so during twenty years of stalking together. Stalking has therefore formed a very important part of my life. My 'apprenticeship' cost me much sweat and tears, and not a little blood, as part of the ongoing process of learning. Deer work has, on the other hand, also given me a great deal. Those who are privileged to work with these lovely creatures owe them something for being able to share their lives. Perhaps this book will represent a small repayment both for myself and for my friends and colleagues in the deer world, who will hopefully also find some of their views expressed in these pages.

Sharing our lives with deer. Alan Lewis and Kestrel watching roe in Dorset. (RM)

Whilst it is impossible to mention more than a few of those people, I must select the following friends, again in chronological order, for the contribution which they have made to my knowledge about deer; as well as for their loyalty, friendship and trust, given so freely over so many years.

Bill Hendy was Forestry Commission Senior Ranger at Exeter Forest, Devon, from 1967 to 1982. I zeroed my first rifle and also shot my first twenty or thirty deer with him, and learned a great deal from his inexhaustible store of countryside lore, as well as from his wicked sense of humour and his ability to take a completely oblique look at life. Bill was prepared to take a chance with me and help me, and for that I shall forever be in his debt.

Alan Lewis first came stalking with me in 1978 to see whether he would like it or not, and has stayed on. I find it impossible to describe his contribution adequately. He is loyal, trustworthy, totally reliable, a good, knowledgable and dedicated deer man, and my closest friend. He also has a wonderful knack of forcing me to come up with clear-cut answers, as well as keeping my feet firmly on the ground.

Eric Masters was Forestry Commission Senior Ranger at Wareham in Dorset until his retirement in 1991. He has a deep understanding as well as a detailed knowledge of the deer in his native country and more to the point he writes it down. His detailed records are a credit to him, and he has been unstinting in sharing his knowledge with me whenever I have asked his advice. I only wish that I had met him years before, and had been able to find more time to learn from him.

Eric Masters in Wareham Forest, 1991. (RM)

Stuart Venables is a full-time deer manager, based in Dorset. He started his own deer management service when he came out of the Navy and we met whilst he was taking the old Advanced Stalkers' Course of the British Deer Society because I was lecturing on that course. Stuart liked some of the things I advocated and he kept in touch, so that gradually we developed a professional relationship, as well as becoming firm friends. Stuart has advised me from the viewpoint of somebody who has to made a living from working with deer, and anything which he endorses is likely to be essentially practical and workable.

Mark Warn, Vic Pardy and Colin Elford are Forestry Commission Leading Rangers in Dorset, and a fundamental part of the deer management team to which I shall refer so often through the book. Colin is an author in his own right, and he encouraged me to 'go for it' when I was given the chance of writing this book. Mark has helped me improve the detail of the text. Vic is another deer man with a knack of asking difficult or penetrating questions, which have required me to come up with better answers over the years. I am also indebted to him for allowing me to use some of his superb photographs.

The way the book is structured

In developing my arguments I shall use quotations from time to time throughout the text in order to illustrate the diversity of opinion about deer which currently exists. These will be shown in inset boxes (frames), and will be published quotes from experienced people within their own professions. It will be for the reader to decide how to interpret these quotes. Some will fit closely with the arguments which I shall develop whilst others will show a different, indeed often opposite view. I hope that this approach will encourage readers to spend some time exploring these different opinions, to make up their own minds, and take nothing for granted.

Deer management is partly art and partly science, and the skill lies in knowing the options which are available and in being able to match selected options with individual deer management objectives. Look at what practicioners and experts alike have to say; see what common ground there is; decide which parts strike a chord with your own experiences and you will be well on the way towards developing a deer management system which will meet your own requirements.

The aims of the book

Deer have for a long time been a central part of my life, and I hope that this book might help in some small way to encourage improvements in their management. I see this in the sense of 'survival of the species' rather than the survival of the individual, and, generally, I am comfortable with that view.

First I want to help deer stalkers, deer managers and those charged with estate management to develop effective and practical approaches to deer management, so that they can devise appropriate solutions to the problems which they might face as a result of having deer on their lands. Secondly I want to help resolve some of the contradictions which readers might come across as they carry out more serious work with deer. And finally I want to set out a series of guidelines which will be adaptable to most situations which readers might encounter as they work with deer in the lowlands.

In doing all this I am not setting out to tell readers what they should do; I am simply describing an alternative approach to deer management, which may help them, whether they are landowners, land agents, forest managers, stalkers or deer managers, to define and meet their own objectives within a general framework of guiding principles.

An important aspect of this approach is realistic and achievable objectives. For my colleagues and me, this has meant a constant reappraisal of our attitudes, which is an uncomfortable process, and one which demands a degree of self-assessment. I find that identifying appropriate and realistic objectives is difficult, and the process of re-appraising and updating them is continuous; but when they are both realistic and clear (which sometimes needs several attempts), they can be set out as short statements which are easy to understand. Achieving those objectives often becomes easier than one might anticipate when everybody involved is clear about what the aims are and what is expected of them. Everything else, then, tends to fall into place. More information about how to select appropriate objectives for deer work is given in Chapter 1.

There should be something here to interest most people who experience the problems which wild deer can cause, but the book is aimed particularly at those who are currently experiencing problems to which they have inadequate or incomplete solutions. This will often be in situations where levels of deer damage, either to trees, crops or habitats, are so high that the viability of those crops and habitats is being threatened, and existing efforts at deer management are failing to bring it under control.

Since there is plenty of easily obtainable information on all aspects of stalking methods and equipment, and since training courses for novice and semi-experienced stalkers are readily available, I shall assume that readers already have some knowledge of these matters, or are prepared to find out more from the appropriate sources. This is not, therefore, a stalking or training manual, nor do I intend to enter a debate about ballistics and equipment. Although these subjects can provide light relief for some stalkers, who argue endlessly about the relative merits of this calibre or that, this bullet weight or that or this or that item of equipment, I personally find that this often distracts attention from the central issue of how we should be managing our deer.

I have found for instance that every legal deer rifle I have ever used, with all the bullet weights I have tried, has killed deer cleanly and effectively when used properly. And I cannot recall ever wondering whether I would have been more successful if only I had had a particular item of equipment or clothing. When I have failed to stalk deer successfully it has usually been because of poorly applied fieldcraft, and occasionally simple bad luck. I do not delude myself that the acquisition of additional equipment will put such matters right – attention to fieldcraft will be much more fruitful. The main point about equipment is that it should be selected in order to do a particular job and when selecting it is useful to be able to distinguish between essential, desirable and luxury items.

Furthermore, it is not my intention to try and 'sell' any particular deer management system. If things are working well for you then it is probably wise not to make major changes; as the saying goes, 'If it ain't broke, don't fix it.' But where problems are being experienced with existing practices, or where owners and agents consider that a different approach may be needed, I hope that I shall be able to provide some answers.

Looking at deer from a forester's viewpoint

I describe myself as a forester by trade and a stalker by inclination. As a forester I work with trees – in fact trees are my livelihood. They may be 'wall-to-wall' conifers, fine broadleaves, hazel coppice or ancient woodlands. They might be managed as an economic enterprise, or for conservation. They may contain a wide range of flora and fauna which depend upon the woodland habitat or be almost devoid of vegetation. But they are all trees, and for many years I have carried varying degrees of responsibility for their wellbeing.

A roe doe in a Dorset beech wood. (RM)

As a deer stalker or deer manager (and I am both), I work with deer. They may inhabit coniferous forests on acid soils or beech or oak woods on alkaline loams, or they may be family groups of roe living in hedges and small copses on farms. They may be different species in different situations, but they are all deer. The struggle for me has been reconciling the woodland habitats and the deer so that they can live side by side in reasonable balance in our modern countryside.

My occupation has meant that I have come up against deer almost on a daily basis for much of my career, often in a confrontational way when I have had to deal with the damage which deer can cause to trees, crops and vegetation. In common with other forest and woodland managers, I have found that there is an abundance of opinion and advice available on how deer should be managed, but those offering such advice often have limited experience of managing woodlands. Much of their advice also has its origins in the way in which they work with deer – at the most basic level, as a sporting resource. Such approaches, based predominantly on sport or recreation, provided the central thinking behind many deer management principles. Many professional stalkers, as well as deer management groups, have therefore become conditioned to think in this way.

I offer a different set of experiences and expectations; those of land managers taking primarily a forestry or woodland outlook, who look at deer from that perspective. I found early in my deer career that if I followed most of the advice available, well intended though it undoubtedly was, I would simply not be able to achieve the objectives in which I was interested – of sustainable woodland management with low levels of healthy deer. Recognising this conflict was quite easy, but sorting through the available information, selecting those aspects which were of use whilst developing other approaches which were likely to achieve my most important objectives, and building all of this into a workable deer management system, took many years. That process is summarised in this book, together with the conclusions that my colleagues and I reached. In following this path it became necessary for us to develop a different way of looking at deer, one which looked primarily at the woodland habitat and then examining how deer could be managed to fit into it.

Culling wild deer – a different approach

Culling or controlling the numbers of wild deer is uncoordinated across much of Britain, with each estate or forest doing what it considers to be best without the benefit of any kind of regional or national overview. The success of the measures adopted is normally judged in terms of how many animals have been killed, with particular reference to the sexes and perhaps the ages of the animals involved. Such information is often useful, and it will always have some value in relating one year's plans and achievements to another's, as well as in developing better and more effective planning strategies. However, if we are to widen our approach to consider how deer impact on the habitat they occupy, a better yardstick might be to try and relate the impact of culling upon damage levels in those habitats – in other words to use deer damage to the habitat to act as the primary criterion in determining the level of culling which is necessary.

Culling is invariably discussed when stalkers meet, because everybody accepts that deer can cause serious problems to forest trees, farm crop, and, in latter years, conservation areas, and this is the main reason why stalkers are needed – to control numbers. The stalker therefore has to be seen to be doing something, and the simple answer is to be seen to be shooting deer. Most discussions about culling therefore revolve around how many need to be shot in the particular circumstances under review, and in order to know how many should be shot, it is necessary to know roughly how many are present at the moment – or so the argument has gone ever since I can remember.

But if woodlands and woodland habitats are important elements in your estate management strategy, then in order to make real progress with your objectives it may be helpful to get out of this cycle of dependency on deer numbers, and concentrate on what is happening to the habitat as a result of deer pressure on it. For the woodland manager the real issue in judging whether enough deer are being shot should be the effect that culling is having, both in terms of natural vegetation and planted crops, rather than, simply how many are being killed. It is really a question of learning to focus on a different objective.

The idea of deer as a sporting opportunity, and therefore as capable of being marketed as a recreational resource, goes back to the 1960s or even earlier, when foreign clients were encouraged to come to Britain to enjoy cheap stalking. It is also easy money, with precious little input being required apart from construction of a lease. Letting deer stalking to a tenant therefore becomes attractive to land agents and owners, but they frequently find that problems arise as a result of this decision which they could not have predicted. Appreciating the knock-on effect on other land management issues (particularly, though not exclusively, woodlands) of the deer management options selected is a subtle and thus frequently overlooked art, but few appropriate, long-term management solutions will be found without a greater understanding of the full range of issues involved.

That is not to say that letting stalking is wrong. I ran a deer management system for the Forestry Commission for many years which maximised income from fee-paying recreational hunters whilst providing them with quality experiences and at the same time minimising deer damage to forest crops. I am, therefore, the last person to argue against recreational stalking, and I would not necessarily even argue against stalking tenancies – certainly where viable woodland management is not important to the landowners. What I do argue against, however, is short-termism – using recreational stalking or stalking tenancies as expediencies without either linking them to overall estate management systems or understanding the knock-on effects when deer management is poorly targeted. In the final analysis this means being able to define realistic objectives as well as developing the ability to put them into practice. Advice on defining such objectives will be given in more detail in Chapter 1.

Counting deer in the wild

A recurring problem for deer managers is that of counting deer in order to work out how many to shoot, since it is difficult to determine how many should be shot unless you know the size of the population at the start. But the fact is that you cannot do so accurately, by any currently available cost-effective techniques. Furthermore, in most circumstances it is of little use even to try. This view is now becoming more widely accepted but if you complain about deer to most stalkers and say that damage levels are too high, the first questions they will ask will relate to the size of the population, as a preliminary step in deciding how many should be shot. I struggled with this problem for years, and even though I now have answers which usually work, they have no clear statistical basis. I therefore have to work hard to defend my ideas because they do not depend on knowing the size of the local population. But since it has proved very difficult to count wild deer with any reasonable degree of accuracy using normally available methods it seems logical to me that figures thus obtained must be approached with extreme caution. Because the cost of gathering them can be quite high, and since it can be misleading when it is obtained, the exercise has an inbuilt potential for wasted effort.

Sticking one's neck out and deciding cull levels without the benefit of population estimates is uncomfortable, but it does become easier as confidence grows. My way of approaching this task focuses much more on habitat indicators and the pressure on vegetation than on knowing precisely how many deer are in the area, and over the years I have become more and more comfortable with it as I have seen improvements to the woodlands which I manage. What is important is to link habitat indicators, deer damage levels and pressure on vegetation with previous culling levels, so that future culling levels can be decided and, if necessary, modified in the light of recent indicator information. My way of doing this is rather rudimentary, and I would certainly use a more objective system of measuring deer impact on habitats if one became available and was reasonably practicable.

Censuses of deer populations were carried out by all of the deer groups with which I have been associated in order to devise annual cull plans and also by the Forestry Commission. They changed that system in Dorset on my recommendation in the early 1980s. But the census technique was widely recommended in the 1960s and 1970s, and has still not yet entirely died out. The theory is fine: as long as you know how many there are, you can decide how many to shoot to manage the population. But if you think it through a little more carefully, you will see that it is not as easy as that. How do you want to manipulate the population? Do you need to reduce it? By how much? How will you know when it is at the correct level, and how can you work out how to maintain this level, or know when changes have taken place which may demand a reappraisal of the situation? What is the annual reproduction rate of the deer under review and how does this change as the population changes? It is a veritable minefield, which is why many of the older generation of stalkers that I knew had no confidence in the approach. Most stalkers are above all practical men, who need guidelines they can understand and follow, and the more complicated the guidelines or the more unreliable the baseline information, the greater will be the potential for error.

For me this has meant coming up with a set of practical guidelines which will fit most situations, and which should be capable of fine tuning in order to achieve the woodland and deer management objectives of particular landowners. Deer managers and stalkers can then be charged with the task of going out and achieving these objectives, and to go on doing so year after year.

To show how these guidelines developed, I shall describe the range of management and stalking tasks that a deer manager may face in a typical year. It will be assumed that this person is being required to achieve management objectives which assume healthy woodlands and associated habitats, together with low levels of deer damage. He or she may be a professional or an enthusiastic part-timer, it does not matter; it is the attitude with which the task is approached that most concerns us.

My recommendations are not always complete, and questions are raised as well as answered. However I believe that the approach I describe represents a significant step in the right direction. It has taken me thirty years to get this far, and if some of the ideas discussed stimulate others to develop them even further, then my effort will not have been wasted.

Planning next winter's cull. (RM)

1.
MANAGEMENT AND STALKING
– THE DIFFERENCES

What is deer management?

This is first and foremost a book about practical deer management in lowland forests, woodlands and conservation sites, rather than about deer stalking. The relationship between deer and woodlands is extremely strong, since they live much of their lives in woodlands, even if they frequently come out onto agricultural land in order to feed. They find shelter, cover, security, breeding terrain and much of their food in woodlands and most of the economically significant damage they cause occurs in woodlands, although of course farm crops and increasingly conservation sites and horticultural crops can also suffer – sometimes seriously.

It is also important to recognise the essential difference between deer management and stalking, as many people confuse them. The distinction becomes important when interests clash, and I will illustrate this with an example. A few years ago on one of the commercial forests where I was responsible for Forestry Commission deer management we experienced severe damage to a crop of newly planted pine trees. The land in question was leased to the Forestry Commission on a long lease, but many rights were reserved to the landowner. One of these rights may have been the right to take deer, although there is considerable difference of opinion about the exact terms of the lease in this respect. From the time that this crop had been successfully established to the start of the clear felling and restocking phase of the forestry cycle there did not appear to have been many problems. Reducing the deer population in advance of clear felling in forest blocks where little control may have been needed whilst the crop was in the semi-mature stages is standard practice in the Forestry Commission, but it had not occurred to us to do so in this particular area because it had an active stalking tenant, and the deer population did not seem excessively high. However, the stalking tenant worked to the landowner's requirements, and not to those of the occupiers, who were managing the land for forestry. The different objectives of the owner and the long-term tenants meant that they had a totally different approach to the deer. This subsequently proved to be a major problem in the negotiations which followed.

The scale and speed with which the damage occurred made it imperative for the forestry managers to exercise what are known as 'concurrent rights', whereby the ranger team was instructed to deal with the problem by shooting some of the offending deer immediately, and this provoked a major storm. It subsequently transpired that the stalking tenant had been *building up* the roe population so that he could enjoy better trophies, and this was being done in a forest where one of the major objectives is growing trees commercially. Without going into further details this incident illustrates what can happen when different parties are acting (quite legally) on the same land, but pursuing objectives which are not compatible. This took some while to resolve, and both parties were caused substantial distress – the stalking tenant and his stalker by having their carefully laid plans turned head over heels in an instant, and the forest managers by having to invest undue time in sorting out the situation, as well as suffering substantial financial loss.

The issue at stake was that the landowner was quite legitimately making money by leasing the stalking, whilst the forestry tenant was picking up the damage bill. This situation could hardly be described as fair or sustainable, especially since the forestry lessees were quite sure from their past experience that they would be able to practise an alternative form of deer management which would minimise such damage. The stalking tenant and his retained stalker were caught in the middle of this dispute; he had paid good money, and was understandably annoyed at having his plans overturned; though equally he was not prepared to pay the costs of deer damage to the forest in return for the freedom to practise his own brand of deer management.

I had not previously come across a stalking tenant *building up* a deer population in a commercial woodland – at least not openly. To a forest manager this would be tantamount to professional negligence, whilst to the stalking tenant it was simply a way of enjoying his investment. The difference could hardly be more marked, and in the final analysis the test was who was prepared to pay for the costs of deer damage.

'If there are ten deer in the same wood, but all the trees are being eaten, eight of those deer may need to be removed.'

Roe in an ancient woodland in Dorset, January 1997. (RM)

Damage to crops is the most important criterion in managing deer. (RM)

Most foresters spend at least part of their lives trying to reduce deer populations to manageable levels in order to protect their crops, and I can easily understand why so many continue to see deer as a major threat. Whilst a greater proportion of foresters probably welcome deer as part of the forest ecosystem, in doing so they tread a tightrope. They need to find a way of accommodating deer in their woodlands, whilst minimising the cost of any damage they do. If you are a stalker operating in an area where growing trees is an important objective you need to realise what the forester's aims are. It matters little whether the trees are for commercial crops, for conservation (say in the form of ancient woodland or coppice management) or for amenity or shooting – if you want healthy trees then you have to have quite low levels of deer. There is no real alternative, and we will come back to this point time and again.

I will illustrate this with another little story. Many years ago one of my forester colleagues was trying to establish a young broadleaved (deciduous) crop in a wood that had only recently come into Forestry Commission management. The wood had a high roe population, and the forester was experiencing a lot of damage to restocked areas. An acknowledged expert was brought in to advise. He explained how the population had built up (which we already knew), how the territorial bucks would 'police' the area, how the damage may not really have been as bad as we thought, and how we must make sure that we were only shooting the offending animals. Finally, the Chief Forester looked up from his notes and said, 'The way I see it is this. If I have a hundred deer in this forest and my trees are fine and I do not have complaints from neighbours, why should I worry? If there are ten deer in the same wood, but all the trees are being eaten, eight of those deer may have to be removed in order to control the damage.' This statement, made under some pressure to get something done, set me thinking and I have never forgotten that lesson. Whilst this view was too simplistic in terms of devising a sustainable, long-term deer management system, it showed absolute clarity because of its essential simplicity. It also focused upon the issue which is central to forest managers, which is damage to crops rather than the size of the deer population.

Whilst some deer managers might be outraged at the thought of such indiscriminate control, to the hard-pressed forester this would be a natural response to the problem. I have tried to develop a much more predictive and sensitive system, but with the same underlying principle of the need to judge the deer population not by numbers but by the damage caused.

That brings me neatly back to the difference between management and stalking. Stalking may be described as the act of outwitting a wild creature on its own terms and observing, photographing or killing it as appropriate. For the purpose of this book I will take stalking to mean outwitting in order to study or kill. The term management implies that some form of control is being exercised by the manager. Both terms can be used legitimately to describe a range of deer-related activities, but it is important not to confuse them. Management also implies defining and achieving objectives whilst the term stalking does not assume this; and frequently defining and achieving realistic objectives can be the most uncomfortable and difficult part of managing a population of wild deer.

Many recreationally orientated stalkers are able to avoid the woodland management issues, and from my experience many land agents and managers are often too busy with other priorities to devote enough time to defining what they really want from their deer management other than a large rent each year. The usual result is that realistic deer management objectives are not set, or that the responsibility to do this is delegated to a chosen 'deer man'. This option can work well when that person is experienced enough to know what the owner wants and how to deliver it. It will work less well when he is less experienced, or has an agenda of his own which may not be in the best interests of the owner. Such situations are often perpetuated because nobody really knows how to go about changing them. In *Forestry and British Timber*, June 1996, for example, Roger Buss, a professional stalker, put forward a commonly held approach to setting culling levels, based upon the theory of natural selection, where old, sick and weak animals succumb, as do a high proportion of juvenile animals. He said: 'The total number culled of any species in a year should not exceed the previous year's fawn survival rate, unless there are obviously too many deer and damage is being caused.' This is accepted theory, but from a woodland manager's viewpoint it makes one assumption which has far-reaching consequences: that in choosing such a management system the manager usually does not need to achieve a reduction in population. If a reduction is required then clearly the annual cull must exceed the previous year's fawn survival rate – otherwise no reduction will be likely. And it is rare, in my experience, for woodland managers to face situations where a reduction in deer numbers is not necessary.

Deer stalkers tend to fall into three categories: those who shoot deer with the primary motivation of controlling their numbers; those who see deer primarily as a sporting resource, with consequent marketing opportunities for recreational hunting; and those who are simply interested in recreational hunting either as paying clients, as tenants of stalking rights or with permission from landowners to carry out deer control. It could also be argued that the first group tend to be motivated primarily by an interest in the management and welfare of deer with a secondary interest in the financial aspects of deer work, whilst for the second group that position is often reversed. The third group is usually simply prepared to pay for the pursuit of its pastime. Obviously that is a sweeping generalisation, and I put it forward for no other reason than to highlight the basic differences in our approaches to deer, and consequently to their management. There is little doubt that their motivations often overlap, so that recreational stalkers will shoot some deer as a control measure, and deer controllers will often accommodate fee-paying clients to help defray expenses. However, the basic difference in approach and motivation is always there, even if it is often submerged; and it is this difference in motivation which we will consider as we explore how deer stalking and management have developed in Britain since the Second World War, and as I develop my ideas of how I think it should continue to develop as we approach the new millennium. It is also interesting to note that, according to the BASC Stalking Survey of 1997, 86 per cent of active deer stalkers are recreational stalkers. 60 per cent have been stalking for under ten years while 2 per cent have been stalking for over forty years.

I shall deal with deer management in much more detail than stalking. I will look at how to define objectives for deer management, how to set targets and how to understand how deer management can affect other aspects of forest, farm or estate management. Since these are tricky subjects to deal with I shall continue to use the term *stalker* to describe the deer culler whilst going about the job of shooting deer, whether he is doing this as part of his occupation or simply as a recreational activity, whether for control or for sport. I will use the term *deer manager* to describe the person (owner, agent, forester or stalker) who has the responsibility for deer management in the wider sense. Obviously, the same individual may be described in different ways at different times, particularly where one individual has more than one responsibility, but the term used will relate to the function being discussed.

I have identified some crucial differences between deer stalkers and deer managers, and I would argue that there will be a greater need in the future for more emphasis to be placed upon deer management than on stalking, or at least for the views of the managers charged with achieving overall estate management objectives to hold rather more sway. Managers, be they land agents, foresters, farm managers or whatever, usually carry a range of responsibilities for overall management, whereas frequently the stalker or stalking tenant only has to consider the deer – and often, then, only in a sporting sense.

In saying all of this I am not suggesting that one is better or worse than the other. That is not the issue. They fulfil different needs and both have their place in the deer world. The important thing is for the managers who carry the responsibility to be clear about what is wanted and to be given the management freedom to be able to achieve it.

This book starts from the premise that the presence of deer, particularly in woodlands, often generates more problems than opportunities, and as we look in detail at what those problems are we will also look at whether there are long-term solutions which are practical and applicable, and what those solutions might be, as well as at areas where deer management falls short of our requirements.

The subject is complex, and understanding the interrelated issues surrounding deer is not helped by the fact that in the final analysis we actually know very little about their ecology, particularly in terms of how they interact with their environment. We know that over the last century they have been enormously successful in expanding their range, distribution and populations in Britain, but much of our current knowledge is based upon field observations by stalkers. Objective research has only recently become available, and then in rather restricted fields which are often of limited use to the small-scale or part-time stalker.

The contributors to this book know that what is described here actually works, but there is not and never will be, any instant solutions. The lessons we have learned cannot be applied rigidly. They must be adapted to local circumstances, and constantly fine tuned; and it is in these areas that the real challenge for deer managers lies. Long may it continue, for if it were easy anybody could do it, and the challenge

Portrait of Dorset

The settlements at Ashmore, Woodcutts and Farnham remained small until the hunting of deer went out of fashion. There are still wild deer in the district, fallow and roe are fairly common, but unless a search is made for them they are seldom seen. They do a certain amount of damage to root crops by pulling up far more than they eat, but the grazing of pasture at night is seldom noticed. The foresters who cultivate trees in plantations find them a bigger nuisance than any other countrymen.

Ralph Wightman 1965

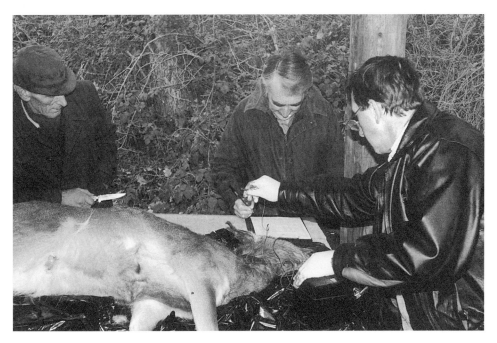

Undertaking deer research. Wareham, 1990. (RM)

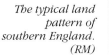

The typical land pattern of southern England. (RM)

would be gone. It is one of the few areas of life today where judgement, skill and wisdom remain essential tools, whilst modern technology and the 'quick-fix' solution play a rather more subordinate role.

I shall attempt to explain how complex it is to manage deer for a range of different objectives, and I shall seek to identify the place of deer in the modern woodland ecosystem, in relation to the habitat which they need to occupy. In doing that it will be necessary to see how their presence impacts upon other legitimate users of that same habitat, including other species of flora and fauna as well as humans. In tackling those issues I shall be dealing with deer management amongst the typical southern English land pattern of farms, towns and woodlands, with the occasional bigger forest here and there, and with a complex pattern of land ownership and management, and so this is very much a book about the lowlands rather than the uplands.

The particular system described in this book has been used successfully across a wide range of similar forest, woodland and farm situations in order to meet the needs of the landowners involved, ranging from the owners or managers of very large commercially run forests to smaller mixed estates where farming and woodland management exist side by side, as well as to owners or managers of nature reserves or conservation sites. The approach to deer has been developed and structured to ensure that we have met the needs of the various landowners for whom we have worked over a period of approximately thirty years.

I will show how this approach can work equally well for a team of professional stalkers who deal with large areas of commercial forest as for dedicated amateurs who operate exclusively on private land, sometimes in small woodlands and sometimes in larger, more commercially orientated forests, and how it has been shown to be adaptable to land which carries varying degrees of public access.

In most Forestry Commission forests and many private estates pressure for public access continues to increase, and this pressure is unlikely to go away as more people demand access to the countryside – too often, it has to be said, without appearing to be prepared to accept much responsibility either for their behaviour or for the countryside itself. More and more people appear to simply wish to enjoy the country, with little thought about the consequences of their actions. It is part of the transfer of urban attitudes to the countryside and countryside managers, like it or not, have to deal with the world as it is rather than as they would like it to be. Public access to land (often unauthorised) is a live and very real issue, and one which all deer managers need to take into account at all times.

On most of the private land where I have managed deer, public access is normally restricted to public rights of way, but wandering ramblers are frequently found in places where they should not be. The problem of public access is often one of safety. There is no doubt that shooting in Britain, including deer stalking has a fine and enviable safety record, but for some years many stalkers have felt that as more and more people become interested in deer stalking as a recreational activity the potential for accidents is also increasing year by year. As the number of full-bore rifles in the countryside increases and as stalking rents and the cost of the activity continue to soar, the pressure to achieve 'value for money' also increases. In those circumstances the combination of sport-orientated stalkers, often with little rural background or formal training, and more people demanding access to the countryside for other purposes makes many experienced deer people fear that it is more a question of 'when' rather than 'if' a bad accident will occur. I shall return to this issue later under training for novice and semi-skilled stalkers, but it is another reason why I have concentrated upon the development of a flexible and locally appropriate approach to deer management which does not rely primarily upon marketing deer as a recreational resource. This is a vital ingredient of the system which I shall describe here, and an important area where I hope that our experience will help others.

The need for an integrated approach to deer management becomes more apparent when we consider the constant changes which are taking place in our countryside, with an increasing need to find ways of balancing more and more demands upon a resource which can be extremely robust yet at the same time very fragile.

Deer in Britain through the ages

In order to understand why we need to manage deer we should understand the basic problems which they can cause. We also need to appreciate why our thinking has often failed to keep up with rapidly increasing deer populations and an ever-changing environment. To do this we need to look at the niche which deer occupy in the countryside today, and to put that niche into perspective it is necessary to take a brief look back at the history of deer in Britain.

During the Middle Ages deer were nearly wiped out in much of central and southern England, with populations just hanging on grimly in the uplands and in a few large tracts of forest across the lowlands. During the last hundred years or so,

Abiding Things

Twice in a lifetime you may see wild deer in the cultivated fields in daylight. There are dozens within a few miles of my home but they lie in the small woods all day.

Ralph Wightman 1962

(His home was at Puddletown, Dorset. Today there would be hundreds of deer within the same radius.)

however, they have proved themselves to be highly adaptable animals, and they have recolonised and extended much of their former range. In addition at least three species which are new to Britain have found niches. In a word they have proved to be survivors. In an age when we hear so much about threatened and endangered species, and indeed about the threatened world itself, it is refreshing to come across such a success story.

Six species currently live wild, and all continue to expand their range in the face of severe and largely indiscriminate persecution, certainly until the Deer Act 1963 gave them some legal protection for the very first time since the Norman hunting laws. Two of those species (red and roe) are indigenous, and fallow have been here for many centuries, probably since Roman times. However many lowland populations, particularly of roe, stem from reintroductions during the last two centuries. Sika, muntjac and Chinese water deer

Red deer are indigenous . . . (RM)

. . . and so are roe.
(RM)

are relative newcomers, their current populations all having grown to present levels from a nucleus of escapees from deer parks, mainly but not exclusively during and after the two world wars. It is likely that deer have never been more numerous or the species at large so diverse at any time in our history, and populations continue to increase steadily.

Why deer are successful

Deer are successful in Britain for two main reasons: first, most herbivorous animals are able to breed rapidly in order to withstand pressure from the predators which regulate their populations; and secondly, since deer in Britain no longer have natural predators there is no check on population increase. I know that a fox will occasionally take a weak fawn, and there is no doubt that dogs kill a few deer each year. There is also some speculation about bigger predators which may lurk here and there. However, even if we put all of the known instances of deer predation together and add a big margin for error, they would have no more than a peripheral effect on population size; less by far than the deer killed on our roads each year. The only effective predator in Britain is man, whether acting legally and discriminately with a high-velocity rifle or illegally and indiscriminately with the poacher's tools of longdog, shotgun or other instrument.

In considering how successful deer have become it is useful to remember that the most important increase in their populations has occurred during this century,

Man – the ultimate predator. (RM)

and is linked to one major change in land management that has occurred during this same period: the big increase in afforestation which has taken place since 1920. Forest cover in the UK is approaching 11 per cent (*1995 Forestry Commission Facts and Figures*), which is a big improvement on the 4 per cent which existed as the First World War ended, but which still leaves us with one of the lowest percentages of woodland in the world, beaten in this dubious respect only by Ireland and the polar regions, and equalled by Denmark and the Netherlands.

Nevertheless, despite the fact that woodland cover in Britain is still very low if judged in global terms, it is the increase from an extremely low baseline that concerns us as we look for reasons why deer are so successful. Many of the deer which escaped from deer parks during and immediately after the First World War found themselves in a countryside where a very acceptable habitat was being created all around them in the form of these 'new' forests (of course in a historical sense the forests were not new at all – Britain was simply reversing the forest decline which had been experienced since the Iron Age, and which had resulted over thousands of years in bringing the amount of woodland in Britain to an all-time low by 1918).

The deer were not slow to exploit this new habitat and their range has continued to expand slowly but steadily as the decades have passed. As their numbers have grown so has the scale of the problems which they can cause, and in many of the very large and developing forests these population increases took place in remote and often impenetrable areas where the deer had a high degree of safety, and where any form of effective control has proved extremely difficult to carry out. It is fair to say that this problem was not foreseen at the time when those new forests were laid out – hindsight, as always, is a wonderful thing. Moreover, the second rotation forests, which are now coming on stream as the older plantations approach the age when clear felling becomes economically viable, are being planned much more with deer management in mind for the future.

A very acceptable habitat for deer. (RM)

Where any species has the potential for uncontrolled expansion, and can exploit that potential free from persecution, a greatly unbalanced situation will occur sooner or later. If uncontrolled damage to a range of crops and habitats is to be prevented then it is necessary to find a balancing factor, and in Britain man has assumed the role of predator, formerly with snares and shotguns and latterly with high-velocity rifles. The need for this is now widely accepted by society at large, though doubtless there are still plenty of people who find it difficult to accept that killing such beautiful creatures can be either necessary or justified – a view which is not held by many who are charged with the responsibility for managing the countryside or making it pay its way, in my experience. They know only too well that deer can cause severe damage to farm and forest crops as well as to horticultural interests and conservation sites, and such damage is common where numbers are not controlled effectively.

How deer stalking developed

Deer stalking continues to increase rapidly in popularity. In the 1960s, when I first took an interest in deer, the British Deer Society was in its infancy and most deer culling on private land was carried out by a few enthusiasts, usually accompanied by detailed management plans together with entirely commendable codes of conduct and aims for the humane treatment of deer. Organisations such as the Forestry Commission, where deer damage was experienced 'at the sharp end' had long realised that deer had the potential to cause serious crop problems, and indeed were often doing just that. Such organisations usually employed their own staff to control deer, with annual population estimates and balanced culling plans being the order of the day.

In those days the distribution of wild deer appeared to be much more restricted than it is today, but the problems were just as acute in the areas where deer existed in reasonably high numbers. Until the early 1960s the method of dealing with them was generally by organising shotgun drives. These varied from quite professional affairs to ones in which the only qualification was to own a shotgun. Results varied accordingly from the relatively acceptable to the totally undesirable. Since shooting deer humanely with a shotgun, as opposed to simply shooting *at* them, is actually very difficult and requires great skill, there tended to be a high proportion of unacceptable suffering associated with shotgun drives, and wounded or crippled deer were all too common. Consequently the use of shotguns on deer gradually became seen as unacceptable, and the 1963 Deer Act brought the issue into sharp focus, when shotgun killing was restricted by law, in respect of both the weapons and the ammunition that could be used. This was the first time that such controls had been introduced in Britain and legal close seasons for deer other than roe bucks and muntjac were introduced at the same time.

Henry Tegner, through his writings and example, had long argued that medium-bore rifles were the best weapons with which to kill deer effectively, and other enthusiasts had been developing this aspect from the end of the Second World War until the late 1950s. Certainly by the time of my early involvement with deer (during the mid-1960s) the Forestry Commission had implemented rifle control and was introducing stalker training, though many of the first generation of FC stalkers picked it up more or less as they went along, with relatively little training. I well remember my old friend and deer mentor Bill Hendy, who was the first rifle-equipped full-time FC Ranger at Exeter Forest in Devon, saying that when he started he had a short training course and then 'they gave me an old .303 and 50 rounds of ammo, and off I went.'

'What scope did you have?' I enquired.

'Scope' said Bill. 'Bloody rifle had an adjustable backsight and a foresight like a steel stanchion. I used to come up the leg, find a spot about halfway up the body and let fly. In fairness I got nearly all of them with the first shot, but that was more by good luck than good management. Nobody worried much about venison income. The idea was to kill the deer, and if that took three or four shots the damaged carcase was seen as expendable. After about six months they bought me a new BSA Monarch .270 with a Pecar scope and I used that equipment until I retired. The scope made it a much more precise tool, and using it made a big difference to my confidence.'

Bill incidentally still holds strong views about shotgun shooting, having done a great deal of this in his pre-FC days. 'Twenty yards – twenty-five, absolute maximum – loaded with SpSG and I'll put them down every time.' And in my early days with him I saw him do just that. 'Never get a cripple or lose a deer if you're close enough'. The problem really with shotgun control was that very few shooters were good enough to get that close to the deer, and short range is vital. The correct ammunition is also vital, as is knowing how your weapon patterns with heavy shot. I have no doubt that the rifle is the tool for the job, and shotgun control thankfully belongs to an earlier generation, and yet I also have great respect for Bill's views and standards.

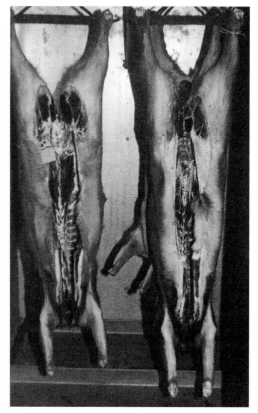

Nobody worried too much about venison income. (RM)

For me, the final conviction that shotguns were by and large unsuitable, came during the early 1970s in Devon, when I was with Bill and shot a sickly fallow pricket one evening. Later, when we were skinning it we found four different sizes of shotgun pellets in the animal – none of which had proved fatal but all of which had contributed to the gradual wasting which the poor deer had suffered. It is very rare to load a shotgun with more than two different shot sizes, so the deer had been shot at with both barrels at least twice. More likely it had been shot at on three or four occasions, possibly many weeks apart. Every shot had been taken well outside the range where a shotgun will kill a deer cleanly, and the result was several extremely painful and debilitating wounds which had crippled the poor animal until its suffering was finally ended by my .270 bullet.

It is important to remember, however, that a rifle does not work automatically, or kill everything cleanly which it is fired at. It is only as good as the person behind it, and I have no doubt that a good shooter with a shotgun will kill more deer cleanly than a poor one with a rifle. Shotguns will play no further part in this book, however. I mention them merely to give a historical perspective and also to reinforce the point that the objective for the dedicated stalker is to become highly proficient when using a rifle on a live target, and to learn not to shoot until he is sure of killing that target cleanly, whatever the weapon being used or the circumstances.

Deer in woodlands – recreational hunting or planned control

A position was reached, probably in the first few years after the Second World War, where deer were being seen as a major pest and a threat to growing woodlands, which had to be exterminated by any means possible. Many woodland and farm managers still hold such views, and although they are seen as extreme and unacceptable today the issue of high deer numbers and unacceptable levels of deer damage simply will not go away. In many areas deer numbers and consequent damage levels are still too high to allow the creation and management of viable woodland habitats, and this is likely to remain the case until we learn how to reduce deer populations so that damage to trees, crops and vegetation are judged acceptable when considering the overall management requirements of those habitats. Once we have learned how to reduce deer numbers to achieve these objectives and we can recognise the point at which this balance is achieved, the next priority will be to maintain them at similar levels and develop better ways of habitat monitoring to determine the required degree of future culling. We are unlikely to achieve these objectives by relying simply on trying to assess deer populations and devising culling plans based upon this approach. This has often been tried in the past, and has generally failed. We need to look much more closely at the habitats which deer occupy and determine culling levels by judging the pressure on those habitats. In doing so we shall have to challenge many of the assumptions which underpinned earlier views on deer management.

In many ways the argument in recent years has shifted. It now centres not on whether deer control is necessary, but more on how much control is needed, who

We must learn how to reduce deer populations to achieve healthy woods. (RM)

should do it, and under what circumstances. In my experience views about this tend to polarise into different camps, depending usually on the viewpoint from which the observer is approaching the subject. As I am a forester with an interest in deer I tend to see the subject primarily from the angle of woodland management, and how deer can fit into viable woodland; rather than how woodlands can be manipulated to accommodate deer. People whose primary interest lies in using deer as a marketable resource will, of course, see this from a totally different perspective. In determining your own response to these potentially conflicting approaches it can be helpful to consider where responsibility for the wider management of the habitat actually lies. For me the person responsible for the area's overall management needs to have the freedom to make decisions relating to that management. Woodland and forest managers often feel that their efforts are frustrated by deer-stalking tenants, who all too often carry no real responsibility for the deer damage which may be a consequence of the particular management system which they have put into place. It is this issue of 'power without responsibility' which frequently invokes anger – when the stalking tenant decides on the deer management system but the woodland or forestry manager bears the costs of deer damage.

Although clearly biased, I see advantages if woodland managers assume overall responsibility for deer management; together with the ability to make the necessary decisions, including the priority which is given to sporting income from deer. It is not fair to ask deer managers who purchase stalking to undertake this since their judgement will invariably be clouded by the overriding need to recoup their investment, rather than the need to achieve effective deer control. However, it could be done by deer managers retained on a different basis – such as on a system where priorities are agreed in advance, and the *risks and rewards of implementing the chosen management is shared between the woodland and deer managers*. I say this with some trepidation because I am constantly staggered by the degree of ignorance about deer demonstrated by so many woodland managers; indeed the total lack of interest often demonstrated about deer until there is a problem – by which time it is usually too late. The modern slavishness towards clearly measurable financial objectives also worries me in this context, because everyone has become conditioned to find an immediate answer or 'quick fix'. This

The cost of preventing or minimising deer damage. (RM)

is not the same as finding the sort of genuine long-term (sustainable) solution so often required when dealing with deer management. However, the many good forest and woodland managers who do understand or who are interested in long-term solutions, will, I hope be motivated by some of the suggestions made in this book. They nearly always, because of the demands of their profession, have two great attributes when considering deer management; they understand management responsibilities and usually have experience in balancing conflicting priorities in a wider context.

A note of caution here revolves around two management approaches which are frequently disastrous where deer are concerned. I have coined the terms 'spotlight management' and 'group think' to describe them. Many organisations are guilty of them, and these days they are often forced into greater prominence because of heavy workloads and the constant need to reduce costs. By 'spotlight management' I mean when management looks carefully at narrow areas of responsibility with the intention of introducing cost-cutting measures or gains in efficiency, without considering the wider ramifications of such innovations. One classic example I remember from my early forestry career involved a study into a timber harvesting operation, where, in order to reduce the cost of extraction (from stump to roadside), the cost of haulage to sawmill increased substantially. The effect was that although one element of the job cost less, the whole operation cost much more.

By 'group think' I mean the desire for many large organisations in particular but not exclusively, to encourage a standardised approach. For producing widgets this is fine, but for countryside management in any form, such an approach can only go so far – at some stage a more individual interpretation may be needed in order to solve a problem. An example which I can give is a recent one. I did a long-term woodland management plan for one of my clients, for a woodland which was also a Site of Special Scientific Interest (SSSI). A great deal of thought went into this, with the intention of hopefully setting out a blueprint for the future. When discussing this with various interested bodies throughout the consultation process which was necessary to implement this plan, a young man proceeded to highlight a potential deer problem and lecture me on how it should be tackled. His highlighting the problem didn't bother me unduly, as I could see that happening as well, and plans were already being laid to get the population under control. What did disturb me was his insistence, *at such an early stage in our discussions* on what should be done. I asked what species of deer lived in that wood, what basis he had for assuming a high population, what kind of reduction he was seeking and what timescale we should be working to. His answer was along the lines of 'I don't know what deer are here, or what damage they are causing. I have never been here before. However, I always assume that there will be problems, and require remedial steps accordingly'. He had clearly read the latest articles on deer management (it subsequently transpired that he had read one of mine, advocating a greater need for control), and was pushing a standard line wherever he went. That, in my view, is almost as dangerous as ignoring a deer problem and hoping that it will go away. We need to make decisions based on knowledge and understanding, and if that means woodland managers and deer managers pooling their knowledge, then so much the better.

The BASC Stalking Survey, 1997, also reveals that 40 per cent of stalking is obtained through friends, a third by payment of a fee or rent, 12 per cent through the stalker's employment and 11 per cent through ownership of the ground or stalking rights. So attempts to market deer as a sporting asset have been very successful and deer are now accepted as a highly prized quarry. That is the positive side of developing deer stalking as a sport, but there is also a negative side to that approach which is often overlooked. Because deer have contributed easy income to estate funds we often forget that 'there is no such thing as a free lunch'. Everything has to be paid for – and the price of easy exploitation of deer for sport has been a large build-up of numbers, with a consequent rise in deer damage or in the costs of preventing or minimising such damage.

Although stalking techniques were fairly well known more than thirty years ago, the interaction between deer and woodlands was far less well understood; indeed this has hardly changed today. The development of stalking primarily as recreational hunting rather than as a management discipline has, in my opinion, contributed substantially to many of the conflicts between foresters and deer stalkers today. Because deer stalking has developed as a lucrative (or what appears to be a lucrative) sport, the idea has arisen that it can be done for nothing or, even better, that a profit can be made from what was formerly a cost. However, things have not always turned out as they were intended. Many enterprises have developed which have concentrated upon marketing deer stalking as a recreational activity; indeed the economics which have been applied make it virtually impossible for those who rent stalking rights to do otherwise. Such market-driven systems have generally failed to address the fact that many land managers (as opposed to sporting managers) see the real issue as one of damage control, and are beginning to isolate and identify the real costs and values of using different options for deer management. As this approach becomes more commonly used it will allow woodland managers to identify the true economic picture in relation to deer management, and this in turn will encourage land agents and estate managers to face up to the real costs which may accrue from managing deer primarily as a sporting resource.

It is my deeply held belief that change is desperately needed, for the deer, for our woodland viability and for those who dedicate their lives to working with deer; but the days of easy options have probably disappeared. If you are responsible for estate management and you choose to adopt a market-driven high-rental system of deer management, aimed at maximising rent, that is fine. However it is then no use complaining if you have severe woodland or agricultural crop damage, or if you are unable to adjust the system to meet the changing needs of the estate. It is really 'horses for

> **Damage to trees by deer is considerably less than it was when I began stalking in the late 1960s. Thanks to modern technology we now have tree shelters and other protective methods to minimise damage.**
>
> **Roger Buss, professional stalker, *Forestry and British Timber*, June 1996**

courses', and the management skill lies in choosing an appropriate deer management strategy which also fits with other estate management objectives. Part of the real challenge in deer management for me was learning to focus on those factors which were really important as far as my particular objectives were concerned.

There is a problem in stressing the need to shoot more deer to stalkers who have not yet learned to look at the habitat for indicators, and also in defending the proper and humane treatment of deer, and their legitimate place in the countryside, to hard-pressed woodland managers who would often simply like to see the threat of deer damage totally removed. But I am convinced that the recreational shooting of deer (which brings in much needed revenue) and the achievement of valid forestry, farming and conservation objectives can go hand in hand. However, in order to strike such a balance, a different approach to deer management is needed, for all too often these days there is real tension between those who manage deer primarily for sport and those who see an overriding need for close control of populations. There is a need to find common ground, for the long-term good of the deer themselves as well as of the woodland habitats they occupy.

The woodland management view is broad-based – it has to be, since woodland managers are responsible for everything which affects their woodlands. Frequently, in my experience, many stalkers see things only from the narrow viewpoint of how things affect their interest. That, of course, is a generalisation, but I shall argue throughout this book that the current approach to deer, which has been designed and fostered by many landowners and their agents, allows very little scope for professional stalkers to find better ways of managing deer, because the system is driven by rent rather than by balanced financial control. It is short-term and narrow, rather than long-term and wide-ranging, and there is a real need to reappraise this approach so as to consider long-term woodland survival and viability rather than simply short-term income generation. As farm and estate incomes continue to decline, and as the perilous state of the timber market experienced in 1998 and 1999 makes cost-effective woodland management even more difficult, such a change in attitude becomes even more difficult to achieve. However, if moving closer towards genuine sustainability is a serious national objective, then ways must be found – and found soon.

> Deer of all species continue to increase both in number and range. The cull [for the region] is roughly 30 per cent higher than it was three years ago. We continue to see damage to crops, both forest and agricultural, and to the floral diversity of the forest. In many instances FE seem to be the only people actively managing deer. Through the Deer Initiative we must continue to encourage the formation of Deer Management Groups.
>
> **T.R. Sawyer, Regional Operations Manager, in *Forest Enterprise Annual Report for South and West England*, 1995/6**

Irrespective of the rights and wrongs of such opposing views, it is clear that there is, at best, a major difference in perception. As woodland managers come under ever-increasing pressure to make their activities cost-effective, they are increasingly going to focus closely on threats to those objectives, and will be looking for ways in which real costs can be identified and apportioned accurately.

I have become convinced that effective deer control is quite possible in small woodlands as well as in large commercial forests, provided that objectives and priorities are made clear from the start and are kept under constant review and that the needs of woodland management decide the priorities for deer management and not the other way around. I can demonstrate this with two simple examples.

The area of commercially run forest which was covered by the team of rangers who worked with me in Dorset was around 16,000 acres (6,500 hectares). That was not the whole of the district, simply the bits over which our team of foresters and rangers had absolute control over the deer. Over that area, with an annual restocking programme of 125 acres (50 hectares) each year, no deer fencing was done, nor were tree shelters used. At any one time around 500 acres (200 hectares) of young plantations were vulnerable to deer depredations. Although some damage was experienced, and there were a few troublesome 'hot spots' – we will describe those in more detail later – by and large deer damage was restricted to around 5 per cent of the crop or less. This programme included tree crops which varied from pine plantations on acid heaths to broadleaved/conifer mixtures on chalk soils, and involved at least three deer species: roe, fallow and sika.

At the other end of the spectrum Alan Lewis and I have been managing a roe population for the last sixteen years on a mixed Dorset estate with quite small broadleaved woodlands interspersed with farmland. In contrast to the full-time professional Forestry Commission ranger team mentioned, Alan is an amateur stalker, but with very considerable experience. I use the term amateur simply

Natural regeneration in small woodlands. (RM)

because Alan does not work with deer as part of his living. In every other way he is extremely professional, both in his attitudes and in the standards which he sets himself and achieves. As a result of this programme of deer management we now have natural regeneration (NR) of a range of native broadleaved species in these small woods where the average size of a clearing is the area caused when a single big beech or oak falls down in a gale. At the outset of the programme it was proving impossible to coppice hazel because of roe browsing. This improvement has been achieved simply by getting the population control right and then keeping it at an appropriate level. Nothing else has changed.

Letting stalking rights is seen on many estates as an easy source of income, and for many years it appeared to be lucrative, very successful and easy to manage. Gradually, however, the effects of inappropriate deer management are being seen in the costs of crop protection or in the form of claims for damage which has been caused by deer. When these costs of holding artificially high stocks of deer are set against the 'easy' income, the latter does not look quite so attractive, and gradually managers are learning to identify the costs of various forms of woodland damage more accurately. That will lead to more closely focused appraisals, which I am sure will lead, in turn, to more demands for effective deer control.

It is rare, in my experience, for the leasing of stalking rights to be accompanied by woodland management objectives which the stalking tenant is required to achieve as part of his deer management activities, and it may be that simply insisting on such objectives could lead to more targeted deer management at a stroke. But many stalking tenants, who have paid handsomely for the privilege of stalking, do not like having objectives imposed upon them other than the ones which they want to embrace, and all too often the consequence is the creation of a conflict between stalkers and woodland managers.

Where deer management is integrated into overall estate management policy in such a way that the real costs and implications of the different available options are clearly identifiable, many of these conflicts disappear, as the choice of appropriate deer management options becomes clearer and easier. The correct identification of the available options, coupled with effective financial control, will lead to greater experience of what it is possible to achieve in different circumstances; and from that will come better and more targeted deer management. That will be good for the deer, ultimately good for the deer stalkers, and also good for woodland management.

The scale of the problems currently being faced in many areas explains why the Deer Initiative was set up. It was largely a response by a partnership of organisations in England and Wales, led by the Forestry Authority, to the ever-increasing number of deer-related problems being found in the countryside. It encourages the formation of Deer Management Groups to encourage cross-boundary co-operation between landowners; but note the emphasis on *deer management*. This is not an attempt to encourage deer stalking; it fosters deer management, and recognises the difference.

I have spent almost the whole of my working life managing woodlands. Then in my spare time I work with deer. My love of deer, the need to find solutions to deer problems and my contact with so many deer people through my occupation, have all encouraged me to develop and try out different ideas, always with the aim of improving deer management in the woods under my jurisdiction. I want to see deer and woodlands existing peacefully side by side, in an interdependent relationship, and if that means imposing an artificial management system in order to achieve it, then I can live comfortably with that.

I am the first to admit that compared with many of my professional deer-stalking colleagues my detailed knowledge of deer is somewhat limited. I have also never been in the position of having to make my living from deer management alone, with the discipline which that situation forces upon one. However, I have been in an ideal situation to learn about deer, and also to draw together the experiences of my colleagues.

It is quite possible that being slightly remote from day-to-day management of deer may have been a strength rather than a weakness, since it allows me to take a somewhat more detached view, and perhaps see conclusions which may not be apparent to those who are closer to the subject. Similarly, because I do not depend on deer for my living, I have a greater freedom to put forward challenging views without fear of repercussion – a freedom whch, used carefully, will encourage a more open attitude in the longer term – I hope. I have also been forced by the discipline of my occupation as a woodland manager to develop clear ideas and solutions to problems, often against a background of confusing and sometimes conflicting opinion. Meeting clearly stated and demanding objectives has been a requirement with which I have become very familiar and the results of such an approach are now apparent in terms of woodland survival. The next stage of this process would be finding more precise ways to measure the impact which deer have on their habitats, and then using these to find better ways of determining effective culling levels.

The essentials of controlling wild deer

The effective culling of female deer has long been regarded as a necessity in most stalking publications. Yet, the scale of the problems which many landowners are experiencing suggests that many stalkers and writers are either paying lip service to this need or failing to appreciate the level of female culling which is necessary in order to reduce typical deer populations.

Let me stress again, *it is only through the effective control of the female population that reductions in deer numbers can be achieved.*

Therefore, if the reduction of the deer population is defined as an important objective of estate manage-ment for whatever reason, then effective control of the female

> I have yet to come across anyone who doubts that deer numbers are controlled by culling females.
>
> **T.R. Sawyer, Regional Operations Manager Forest Enterprise S&W(E), 5 July 1995**

Every doe is the mother of a potential trophy buck. (RM)

population becomes an essential requirement, and this is equally true if a primary management objective is simply to hold a population at around its present level rather than actually reducing it. In this case of course the level of female culling should be slightly reduced. For many estate management objectives I would say that a reduction in deer populations should be seen as a normal requirement rather than as an exceptional one.

Many recreational stalkers take the opposite view and believe in supporting a large female population on the basis that every doe is the mother of a potential 'trophy buck'. Often such a view also encourages supporting a high male population as well. This, of course, is because they are primarily interested in managing their deer for sport rather than for woodlands and it is in this important area of population control that the main friction point between such opposing views of management occurs.

My experience suggests that shooting male deer has virtually no effect upon the size of most deer populations, although it may have a very marked effect upon the quality of those populations. The effective control

> **For all species of deer the culling of males should only present problems to the serious stalker in exceptional circumstances. Females present a more difficult problem. The effect of a few days when weather makes outings impossible can throw an intolerable burden upon the part-time stalker, and professionals are not immune from these effects either.**
>
> **Roger McKinley, *Countryside Monthly*, January 1984.**

Deer management – or deer stalking? (RM)

of the female population is therefore the single most important element of deer management when pursuing many woodland management objectives. Understanding this essential fact is the first requirement of aspiring stalkers. It calls for a major shift in attitude towards seeing deer stalking as a management exercise rather than as sport – although clearly there is no reason why the work cannot be enjoyable, and it certainly represents a very big challenge. I forecast that more and more stalkers who operate in woodlands will be required to make this quantum leap in attitude as pressure on the habitats by artificially high levels of deer continues to increase. If I were to be granted a single wish in terms of improving deer management, it would be to see every novice stalker blessed with the ability to see past the trophy to the real achievement of stalking – the outwitting of a wild quarry in its own habitat and under its own terms. It is also critically important that aspiring stalkers should understand the fundamental difference between deer management and deer stalking, and although both approaches may be appropriate in different circumstances it is important for managers to recognise some of the implications of choosing management over stalking or vice versa.

The reason why control of female populations continues to remain so often neglected, is, of course, quite clear: stag and buck stalking remains marketable, whilst few fee-paying sportsmen seem prepared to undertake the very hard but vital work of controlling the female deer population. Those with the most balanced approach, who realise the importance of effective culling, often lease stalking rights and then employ somebody else to undertake the hard graft of the female cull; others simply leave this to chance. How to identify what is required and then to achieve that vital female cull will be discussed in some detail later in the book.

The costs of inappropriate deer management

The need to define objectives accurately was acutely brought home to me when I was the Forestry Commission's Private Woodlands Forester in Dorset during the mid-1980s. Almost every grant scheme I negotiated which involved planting or restocking young trees highlighted potential deer problems. It was my practice to ask what problems might reasonably be anticipated during the establishment stage of any new or replacement crops, and the answers I received invariably involved deer and potential or known levels of deer damage.

I would usually ask what the owner or forester planned to do to resolve these problems so that the trees had some chance of success. The answers were frequently along the lines of, 'Well, we have a stalker.' My response, somewhat tongue in cheek, was that having a stalker was not answering the question. Did the owner know what the stalker did? Had the potential problems been discussed with him (usually yes), and had solutions been decided upon (usually no). Did the owner know how many deer were being shot, and what sexes? Did the owner see any accounts? Did the owner get an annual report? Did the owner discuss targets with the stalker, and were these being achieved? Was this system meeting the owner's needs? Was the stalker using fee-paying clients as part of the adopted system? The answer to most of these questions was usually no, but many owners or agents would argue that the stalker was paying quite handsomely for the stalking, and that the income was a useful addition to estate or farm funds.

When asked about how much money owners spent annually on tree shelters or deer fencing, the answers were often much clearer and relatively large sums of money were frequently mentioned. I often got the impression, however, that many of those with whom I discussed the matter failed to see the immediate significance of the question, which for me was a natural one. Since deer eat or fray trees, thus reducing the viability of the tree crop, the issues of the size of the deer population and the annual expenditure on tree protection are closely linked. If by managing one more successfully the cost of providing the other could be substantially reduced then such options must be worth considering.

In fact, although tree shelters are commonly said to have revolutionised small woodland management, they have in one sense clouded the deer issues considerably. It is true to say that they do provide effective protection and an alternative to deer fencing, albeit at substantial cost, but their widespread use reinforces the view that deer damage is inevitable, so it is as well to protect against it. If this is indeed the case, then the cost of tree shelters should really be shown as a debit on the deer account, since the main reason for providing them is to prevent deer damage.

This brings me to the next problem: to the financial aspects of deer stalking and management. On many private estates deer income commonly seems to show up in the sporting accounts, whereas the costs of tree shelters or fencing come out of the forestry or woodland account. I think that this approach, although simple and convenient, causes more problems than it solves. When this happens, there is no obvious connection through the accounting system between the cause of the problem and the costs associated with solving it. Frequently the forestry department is blamed for its high costs, whereas in reality it had little alternative in responding to a situation forced on it by the deer management option which had been selected.

If financial control is organised so that all transactions relating to deer are located in a separate deer account, then the advantages and disadvantages are identifiable within a single set of figures. It then becomes much easier to see how different deer management options might affect the overall equation.

Defining objectives for deer management

The main issue is to decide what is most important for the landowner or manager of the land. Objectives can vary widely, even for deer management in woodlands, and three examples will illustrate this.

In the large forests of Dorset where I have worked for many years the objectives where deer are concerned are simple. Essentially they are to contain damage to forest crops at acceptable levels (and in recent years we have defined what these levels should be) and to reduce the costs of carrying out this work whilst maintaining the quality. This must be achieved in forests which have considerable public access, and therefore public safety, which is of paramount importance, is a complicating factor. The Forestry Commission employs full-time wildlife rangers who are professionally trained, but while this is a very efficient, highly effective and sensitive system which meets all the defined needs, such professionalism does not come cheaply, and close financial control is necessary in order to ensure that the operation is both cost-effective and also represents affordable and effective insurance. A secondary objective is to respond to neighbours' complaints about deer, where the deer which cause the problems live in the forest, and where the responsibility for controlling them falls on the forest managers.

On a private estate where I have carried out the deer management for many years, on the other hand, the objective when the work started was simply to reduce the numbers so that browsing pressure on the mainly native woodlands was reduced and farm crop damage similarly controlled. And on a third area where I have managed deer for many years the owners simply wanted to be able to show that they had a modern, efficient and discreet system of deer management in place which could deal with complaints from tenant farmers, whilst being low profile in the local community.

So here were three very different situations and three very different solutions required. In fact the management system which will be described later covered all these varying needs quite effectively. Here are some more examples of possible objectives which may apply to various deer management situations, and which may help in clarifying your own ideas.

- to maximise short-term income from leasing deer stalking
- to maximise medium- and long-term income from leasing deer stalking
- to eliminate deer damage (probably unachievable)
- to reduce deer damage to less than X per cent of trees on planted areas which are less than 5 years old
- to reduce deer damage on specified habitats to levels which are acceptable
- to manage deer so as to optimise the balance between the generation of income and damage control
- to ensure that deer damage does not rise above defined levels
- to prevent new species from colonising the area
- to permit cut-over coppice to grow and allow native trees to regenerate successfully
- to produce quality trophies for hunting clients
- to achieve a male:female cull ratio of not less than 1:1.5 each year

These examples illustrate a cross-section of common deer management objectives, both for woodland management and for stalking. Care should be taken in interpreting some of them because other factors may be involved. For example the coppice and natural regeneration objective requires attention from both the deer manager and the woodland manager, preferably working together.

The main thing is to understand the importance of defining, reappraising and updating your objectives, whether financial or for deer management, so that they meet the needs of land managers and landowners, in their own circumstances, and can be easily understood by everyone responsible for their implementation.

Short-term income or long-term performance

Let us now take a brief look at another distinction, this time a financial one: the difference between short-term income maximisation and long-term financial performance.

In most areas of life short-term gain is easy. It simply means capitalising on opportunities (such as accepting a high offer for deer stalking) with little thought for the future. It can work, especially if quick generation of income is the main aim; but more often than not it leads to problems later. In deer management it is the equivalent of the 'boom – bust' economic cycle. Good long-term performance – at least where deer management is concerned – means balancing a requirement to get a desired level of income with another, equally important requirement: to minimise the cost of protection against deer damage as well as the cost of the damage itself.

To achieve such performance means selecting priorities carefully, reappraising them regularly and changing them if necessary. It also means a high level of commitment from managers and stalkers, and can be an uncomfortable process which demands regular assessment. Results do not come overnight. They take time, but are usually sustainable and reliable, and the potential gains can be considerable. In fact, if achieving the best possible balance between increasing income and reducing expenditure is an objective, then significant progress has been made by Forest Enterprise across South and West England in recent years, and my experiences in managing a Dorset roe population free from the pressure of achieving maximum short-term financial targets has allowed the development of what is likely to be a highly sustainable deer management system for small wood management.

Future training needs

Most of what I have so far discussed reveals, perhaps more than anything else, a clear need for education about deer and woodland management and their interface, and such education is needed in my opinion at various levels. By this I mean real education, not simply a cosmetic attempt which will be worse than nothing. To date

Flowchart explanatory notes
In this context public opinion means how important it is for landowners to recognise and take into account local (and possibly national) opinion, in respect of both legal use of the land in question and more general public attitudes towards deer management and other rural issues.

Damage means damage to woodland trees, vegetation or rare habitats as well as to agricultural or horticultural crops.

Income not overriding means that maximising income is not a primary requirement of the landowner as far as deer management is concerned. An example could be where a landowner wanted deer control or management carried out at no cost, but without any of the potential problems associated with recreational hunters or syndicate stalking – perhaps by a local stalker in a low-profile manner, on a shared-income basis.

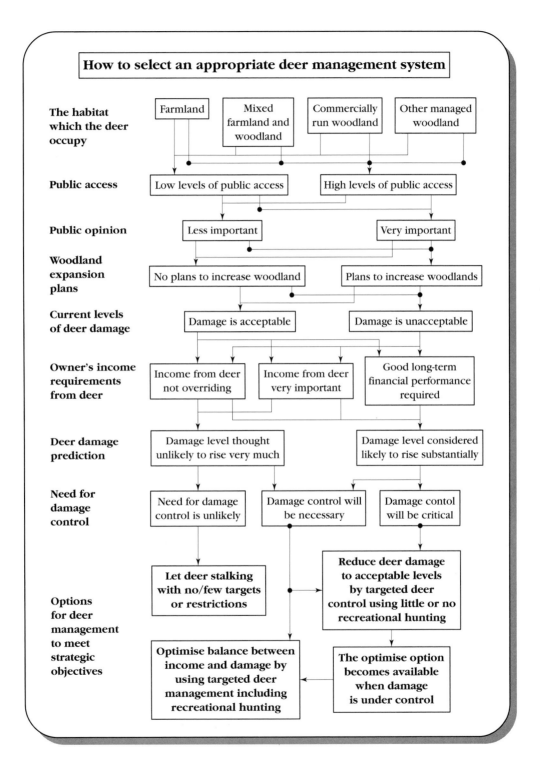

we have proved very good at all the 'fun bits' (teaching people how to shoot, what gear to acquire, and how to recognise deer) but we have been much less good, in my experience, at teaching management principles and priorities for deer in woodlands which actually work in practice. *We are conditioned to see deer as a sporting opportunity rather than as a management challenge.* Consequently, what usually happens is that many woodland managers have little or no understanding of deer (other than the damage which they do), and many stalkers and deer managers have little understanding of woodland management. The educational challenge as I see it has three levels:

Land agents
- to understand how to recognise deer problems, assess whether current solutions are working, and if necessary to set new priorities and offer clear advice to landowners and clients
- to be proficient in setting realistic deer management objectives to meet landowners' needs, across a wide range of circumstances
- to recognise the value of sharing 'risk and reward' with woodland and deer managers, for the overall good of woodlands and estate management
- to recognise the difference between a deer manager and a stalker, and know where to use each to best effect

Foresters and woodland managers
- to acquire a basic understanding of the complexities of deer management in woodlands, as well as the relationship between deer and woodland management, and to be able to set appropriate priorities in order to achieve landowners' objectives
- to understand the importance of 'getting deer management right', or at least 'getting it acceptably right'

Deer managers and stalkers
- to acquire an acceptable level of understanding of woodland management, as well as understanding the interface between deer and woodland management
- to understand the woodland managers' priorities, and to be able to relate deer management priorities to them
- to be able to monitor the effect of deer on vegetation and habitats
- to know when deer control is necessary, and how to set effective culling levels
- to understand how and where recreational hunting can fit into overall woodland deer management priorities, and to be able to reasonably predict and advise owners and agents on the financial implications of chosen methods of deer management.

The next question is who should do such training. As more people become interested in stalking and are looking for somewhere to carry out their hobby, and as sales of full-bore rifles for deer control continue to increase, the need for effective stalker training is obvious. Stalker training has been rather patchy, with various organisations and in some cases individuals offering training courses of varying value. I would like to see this effort co-ordinated, and training made available throughout Britain to centrally approved standards. Ideally, the standards should be agreed by all the organisations with an interest in deer and provided through a single recognised body which would have the confidence of both official bodies (government, police etc.) as well as landowners, deer stalkers and the forest

Stalker training. A BASC training course. (RM)

and woodland industry. In addition I would like to see carefully targeted training for all who have an interest in deer management, in order to help them set and achieve long-term objectives, as well as effectively overcoming short-term problems.

For me the central issue is not who actually carries out the training, but the necessity for a fully integrated approach which can gather information from many sources, disseminate it and develop codes of best practice in differing situations. It seems likely at the time of writing that the recently introduced Deer Management Qualifications Ltd (DMQ) may go a long way towards meeting those needs. It has drawn experience from such organisations as BASC (British Association for Shooting and Conservation), Forestry Commission, Red Deer Commission, British Deer Society and St Huberts Club, as well as the colleges offering specialist courses in deer management such as Sparsholt in Hampshire and many professionals within the deer world. It may prove to be an appropriate organising body, but to meet the needs which I have outlined, deer management, as opposed to sport has to be given a very high priority; and that is the area where so many previous attempts have fallen down. Contributing organisations such as BASC, for example, are primarily sporting organisations, and if effective deer *management* training along similar lines to those suggested in this book becomes accepted as the way forward, they may have to adjust their approach more towards management than sport. There seems absolutely no reason why such bodies could not do this, as long as they see that this is what their members require. There is also a lot of information about the nature and scale of deer problems within organisations like the Woodland Trust and English Nature as well as many county Wildlife Trusts, and much information about deer themselves may be available from localised deer management groups. The vital need as I see it is for an organising body such as DMQ to get a grip of this situation, gather appropriate information, devise appropriate levels of training, preferably with a modular approach, and move forward with confidence. Please note, that in offering those remarks I am directing my observations much more towards deer management and not simply stalking.

Deer management has the potential to be a positive force in the countryside, but a co-ordinated approach to deer in the modern countryside is vital if we are to move forward and face the challenges of that changing countryside, as well as cope with the safety issues which are posed by ever-increasing demands for public access. These pressures are not going to go away, so the challenge is to devise effective solutions to enable the deer manager to continue to do his job in this rapidly changing world. Targeted training has a vital part to play in that process.

There is currently much discussion about linking deer training with the National Vocational Training (NVQ) system, and in my view this approach has much to commend it. Qualifications thus gained would have a nationally recognised value, and would, presumably, be equivalent to qualifications at the same level which are gained in other disciplines. The higher the qualification which is gained, the more the holder would have demonstrated suitability to work at higher and more demanding levels within the chosen subject. This is long overdue, and desperately needed, because if we are to see *deer management* prosper and thrive, then the training, experience and skills of the deer manager need to be seen in the same light as the skills of other managers in different occupations. That would introduce a national standard to deer training, and if this were to be coupled with a national overview of UK deer management, then real progress would be in the making.

2.
SPRING FOR THE WOODLAND DEER MANAGER

Spring is probably the highlight of the woodland deer manager's year, similar to the period which follows harvest in the farming year. The hard work is out of the way for the moment, and there is time to stop and think.

Stopping and thinking has always been very important for me. It means reappraisal; a chance to work out how well, or badly, things are going, and what changes may be necessary for the future. As I get older I find that I value these times more highly. A feature of modern life which I find faintly disturbing is that many organisations seem to have lost sight of the value of 'thinking time' – if you do not appear to be busy, you cannot be doing anything useful. Obviously there is a world of difference between simple time-wasting and vital planning, although to the external observer the outward manifestations may seem similar, but thinking time remains vital as far as I am concerned; both in terms of reappraisal and also of rejuvenation or recharging one's batteries. Where deer are concerned, spring is a wonderful time. Very little shooting is really necessary, the hard graft of the winter culling programme is over, and the deer manager has time to reflect on the past season, and to plan for the next one. Make the most of this time – it is all too short. There are highseats and deer glades to be maintained, stalking paths to be cut, and a host of other jobs to be done, but for the moment the pressure of culling is off.

Looking back

The first stage of the spring programme is a careful look at the past winter's stalking achievements. It is during the winter that the really important work of deer control is done, and it is unfortunately the area which is often most neglected. Never let anyone persuade you that you can control a deer population effectively in any other way than by shooting sufficient females – whatever the species you are concerned with. Shooting males may be very enjoyable, and may put a trophy on your wall, but the hard and demanding part of a stalker's job is demonstrated by how well he keeps on top of his female cull. Forcing yourself out of bed on a January morning when the wind is howling in the eaves is never easy – but if you really want to be a good deer manager you have to force yourself, and this retrospective analysis of the winter's achievements will confirm how successful you have been.

Counting deer

Spring counts have always been a traditional part of accepted deer management principles. In my early days with the Forestry Commission everybody involved with deer had to complete a count, or census as it was commonly known. The results of this census formed the basis of the next year's culling plans. If you wanted a comfortable life you instructed your rangers to carry out a census, transferred the results onto an annual return, made an estimate of road casualties, likely mortality from other causes, shooting around your boundaries and poaching, and at the end of this process made your estimate of the next year's proposed cull.

Like many people, I was rather naive in my early days, and I believed in the obvious value of counting deer. Gradually, however, I began to see what was actually happening rather than what was supposed to be happening. Bill Hendy cast the first doubts in my mind when I asked him one day about deer counting. By this time he had come to trust me and probably realised that I was genuinely trying to make improvements, and he was quite forthright. 'How many deer on my patch? I haven't got a bloody clue, boy.' I was horrified. Here was I, supposed to be in charge of managing these deer, and we were shooting substantial numbers each year. Yet Bill was saying he had no idea of the size of the population. Furthermore our plans were based upon the results of this count and I was signing the return which was submitted each year.

'How do you arrive at your cull plan, then?' I asked.

Census

Having calculated the holding capacity, it is necessary to find out the numbers of deer on the ground. For roe in small areas, this can be done over a period of weeks by an individual observer. For red, fallow and sika liable to move throughout their range, the census is best done over two or three consecutive days using sufficient observers to cover the whole range. The use of helicopters or light aircraft with skilled observers would be ideal. The census should be taken by mid-April for lowland deer. By then the bulk of the seasonal deaths from disease and malnutrition will have occurred; roe bucks will have established their territories and red/fallow/sika will have split into separate herds.

Census figures should indicate totals of males and females with an additional record of mature females of breeding age. Only experience can suggest what percentage must be added to account for deer not seen. It may vary from as low as 5 per cent for hill red deer to as high as 100 per cent for roe in thicket-stage woodlands. Especially with woodland deer the tendency is always to underestimate.

The late Lt-Col R.H.A. (Jock) Cockburn, Head Ranger, Forestry Commision, in *Shooting and Stalking*, edited by Charles Coles

'Pretty much guesswork, boy,' he replied. 'I look at last year, add a bit or take a bit, depending how many deer I have been seeing, multiply the answer by the coefficient of friction, take off the square of my mother's birthday – well you get the idea.'

'How do you justify your culling figures then?' I asked, not at all sure that I was going to like the answer to that one either.

'Well now,' Bill answered, 'whilst roe populations are fairly reliable and reasonably static [based on relatively small territories] fallow range over large areas. They can be here today and gone tomorrow. I may be overrun at one part of the year and have none, or very few, at a different time. You tell me, what is the point of trying to get any meaningful count in those circumstances?'

'But you do give me an annual return don't you?'

'Of course I do. Otherwise you'll be on my back like a ton of bricks. I put in figures to keep everybody happy. In fact you're the first forester for years who's ever shown a real interest in what I was doing.' A wicked grin spread across his face, and I listened in some trepidation for what was to come next. As it turned out, it was a pearl of wisdom, and one which set me off on a different way of thinking, and which has led ultimately to the production of this book.

'I look at the damage to trees, and at feeding pressure on herbage, I listen to genuine complaints from neighbours, I use my eyes to get an idea of the deer that may be about, and then I put in a cull figure which I think I will be able to get.' This idea, of looking at the habitat, and not concentrating too much on actual deer numbers, has been a central plank in my deer management strategy over the twenty-five years which have passed since that conversation, although I actually disagreed strongly with Bill over the way in which he decided the cull. I later found that it was a common approach with FC rangers, however. They worked on the basis that since the organisation tended to judge achievement by end-of-year figures, which were seen as the best measure of performance, it was asking for trouble to put in figures which you would not be able to achieve, no matter how compelling the case for doing so. Many foresters agreed with this approach, presumably using the 'anything for a quiet life' approach.

'It keeps everybody happy,' Bill said, 'and what's wrong with that, eh? Nobody ever minds if you get more than you planned for. The problem comes if you get less, so why make more problems than you have to, eh?'

When I look back I realise that this was a turning point for me. I decided then that there must be a better way of approaching this subject; one where motivation would come from a job well done rather than from adjusting the system to suit the circumstances. Given unrealistic expectations or target setting, people will often simply adjust the system rather than try and deal with the unrealistic expectation itself, and so the problem continues. I went home that night with the realisation that I was running a deer management system based on an annual census which was considered nearly worthless by the person doing it, and where the final cull figures were more a representation of what the stalker thought he could achieve, rather than what he thought was necessary. The approach is very different these days, certainly as far as Forest Enterprise in the south of England is concerned, but more about that later.

I steadily became more and more concerned that so many decisions were based on census figures and I was becoming aware that most of these population estimates were at best inaccurate and at worst misleading. My problem is not having to live with insufficient or inaccurate information – that is par for the course in an industry like forestry – it is trying to base precise solutions on possibly inaccurate base data. This can be further compounded by not recognising the potential errors of such an approach and failing to allow for them.

If you complain to most stalkers and say that damage levels are too high, the first question they will ask will relate to the size of the population, and how many need to be shot. It is a perfectly natural question, and yet with current levels of knowledge there is simply no real answer. For a workable answer we must look elsewhere, certainly until more accurate and cost-effective ways of counting wild deer are developed – and I think that this will take a very long time, if it is ever achieved.

The opinion of many deer managers, including myself, is that in woodland conditions there is simply no readily available way to get reliable estimates of populations which are within acceptable margins of accuracy and costs of collection. Numbers are invariably underestimated, often by 200 or 300 per cent. Methods which have been tried include helicopters and light aircraft, observers at vantage points, transect routes, tagging deer or fitting them with highly visible collars, night counts and more recently the use of highly sophisticated night vision and thermal imagery equipment. But most stalkers simply do not have access to either the resources, or the skilled helpers to make use of such facilities. If you

Observers at vantage points. (RM)

have, and believe that it is money well spent, then that is fine. I see such innovations as possibly being valuable when, for whatever reasons, it becomes necessary to produce census figures; or perhaps where a number of neighbours are prepared to combine resources and share the costs of a survey – perhaps to establish a baseline for future deer management. In most circumstances, however, it will simply be too expensive to use such techniques – although as their use increases, their accuracy may improve and the costs drop.

During the last decade, some deer researchers have been looking at the idea of dung or pellet counting. The logic behind pellet counting is that if you are able to predict their decay rate after they have been deposited, and if you have an acceptable method of counting, then it becomes possible to estimate the population from the dung deposits in your study, and thereafter to monitor and calculate population trends. It is still necessary for a number of assumptions to be built in, such as the rate with which the deer deposit their pellets. I am afraid that I still see many problems with this approach, although I can understand the logic behind it and see an immediate application in large, semi-mature (usually upland) forests where access is limited and crops are impenetrable, and where it becomes very difficult to get even the slightest idea of deer populations. But I am as yet not persuaded that the idea is worth pursuing in the more typical woodland and farmland conditions where I manage deer in the south. My main reason for taking this view is simply that the introduction of such a system would have a substantial cost associated with it, and in a financially marginal activity such as deer management I would resist any attempt to increase my costs unless I was reasonably sure that there would be consequent savings of a comparable amount in the future. I am also not convinced that results are any more likely to be accurate than from other methods.

Those costs would rise in two ways: first as a result of the time spent in doing the fieldwork (which is not inconsiderable); and secondly because some routine deer work would not be done as a result of using that time to count dung. Then there are the costs of analysis, and of interpreting the information gathered. Looking at this from the viewpoint of a manager, I would be prepared to accept such substantial additional costs only if they were offset by increased efficiencies or would lead to measurably better results. I can see no evidence to suggest that the adoption of such a system in lowland woods, would lead to either, other than in exceptional circumstances. If I look at this from the viewpoint of an amateur stalker with very limited resources, I would only be likely to take such a demanding system on board if there were the likelihood of a clear return for my outlay of time and money.

Another technique for estimating deer populations is what is known as cohort analysis. The basis of this technique is to analyse jawbones from culled deer in order to establish the age of each beast, and then to plot the ages of the deer shot each year along a line. Since the age of the beast is known, its year of birth can easily be calculated, and therefore recruitment into the population can be plotted. In this way population trends may be ascertained, and predictions made for the future; as long as culling is carried out randomly with no attempt to systematically select certain age classes. The disadvantage is again the cost of carrying out this work, as well as the difficulty in actually getting the jaws analysed. For large organisations this may, in time, prove to be a useful technique, but for most smaller-scale deer managers it seems likely that it will remain largely unavailable because of the costs and potential difficulties involved.

A final cautionary note about the practical difficulties involved in meaningful deer counting concerns a recent attempt by a very sound and practical professional stalker to carry out a census of a particular wood. He enlisted the help of a band of around thirty experienced deer people, who were placed at strategic points around the wood. They recorded all deer seen, the make-up of the groups, the species, the sexes, the direction they were travelling and any other relevant information. At the end of the day the information was pooled and collated, and an assessment of the population was made at around 270 deer. The stalker felt that this was a sound assessment. A few days later the area was visited at night using a highly sophisticated piece of night vision equipment. The lowest assessment of the population based upon the actual count of deer by this method was 460.

All this does not mean that I am against counting deer. I am in favour of anything which helps our understanding, and improves our management of deer. The examples which I have mentioned here (and many, many more) simply reinforce, for me, the rapidly growing view that when managing deer on large or diverse areas of land, the possibility of getting accurate or even reasonably accurate information about deer populations, at acceptable cost, is small with currently available techniques. I have become convinced that rather than to continue to put major efforts into deer counting methods, better progress could be achieved by approaching the subject from a different direction – that of identifying the pressure which deer inflict upon the habitats they occupy, and then in monitoring changes in pressure as populations are managed differently. If easy methods of habitat assessment were developed, they would have widespread application, be cost-effective and provide evidence of a constantly changing picture. To put the difficulties of carrying out an accurate census into clearer perspective, I now list the information which is typically needed:

- You would need to know what species of deer inhabited the land.
- You would need to obtain an accurate count of the resident population, and relate all other information to this base data.
- This information would have to be constantly updated.
- You would also need to be sure whether the area under your census or jurisdiction formed the whole, or only part, of the home range of the deer under study.
- It would be very helpful to know how many deer were being shot by other stalkers within that home range.
- You would need to know whether the herd was being poached, the extent of road deaths, and other ways in which the size of the population was being affected.
- You would need accurate information about the reproductive potential of the herd, and how this might change with various culling levels and how survival to breeding age is affected by culling and other pressures on the herd.

You may have the resources to collect such information, collate it and keep it constantly updated, and you may feel that by doing so you will be a better deer manager. I do not – or rather I feel that I can serve the cause of deer better by concentrating on other issues which yield more useful results. At the end of the day it is up to the individual's priorities and needs, but I was still looking for a viable alternative to counting deer when I arrived in Dorset, and first met Eric Masters.

Eric is a recognised authority on sika deer who co-wrote the British Deer Society's *Sika Deer* publication during the late 1970s, and his knowledge of the deer of his native county is very deep. There are not many questions about deer to which Eric will not be able to provide an answer. It was his practice to spend the whole of March carrying out census work. I know because I used to sign his time sheets. One day, after I had got to know him, and after I think he realised that I was trying to do my best for deer, I asked him why he did this, as it was costing a lot of money, and as a manager it was my job to justify that expense. He did not reply, so later I asked him again. Still no reply. I changed the question. 'Eric, what value do you place on all this census work which you do every year?' I asked.

'Very little.' This was from a man who could probably recognise every stag and buck, and many of the females, on his beat. I tried once more. 'Well why do you do it then?'

'Because I've been told to. Standing Instructions.' Since this answer took me back to square one I tried a different tack. 'What would your reaction be if I told you to stop doing this formal census work?'

'I would be delighted. Then I can use the time to maintain highseats and do all sorts of other jobs which tend to become neglected.'

'What about the value of the deer count. Would our deer management suffer as a result?'

'I don't think so,' Eric replied, after weighing this up for a while. 'Let me think about it and we can discuss it again later.'

The conclusion we reached after much deliberation was that it was a risk worth taking. My next step was to get approval from senior management to stop doing this formal census work. The reasons which I put forward were basically these:

- The knowledge that a dedicated deer manager builds up over the year gives a useful rule-of-thumb estimate of deer populations. This information is gathered as a result of carrying out normal deer work during the year, and does not cost very much to accumulate. This appealed to me as the financial manager for obvious reasons.
- There was nothing to suggest that spending a lot more money on more detailed census work was likely to lead to better results and Eric, like many other full-time rangers, had serious doubts about the value of the annual census.
- The time saved could be put to better uses.
- Too much attention to numbers of deer tended to divert attention from the real deer issues, that numbers were generally much too high, that habitats were suffering and that commercial crops (agricultural or forestry) were at risk.
- If we looked at a 'worst-case' scenario, and actually culled too many deer as a result of not knowing the size of the population (which was what many experts in the 1960s and 1970s were warning against) what would happen? In our view, in the 'soft south', where climatic factors are not normally acute, the population would soon recover if culling pressure were eased. In any event we felt that most of the people who were basing

management systems on estimates of deer numbers were doomed to failure because of the impossibility of getting accurate figures of wild deer in large woodlands.

- Getting ourselves out of the cycle of dependency on censuses might give us the opportunity to look at alternatives.

It would be fair to say that everybody involved in stopping formal census work at Wareham was rather nervous, because from a 'political' viewpoint, census work had some value in persuading the general public that FC deer culling was both necessary and carefully carried out. Furthermore I was making what was effectively a public declaration of my intention to stop this work, and in doing so was taking a considerable risk with public perceptions. And since public perception is a factor which is here to stay, justifying what one does in the countryside to a potentially hostile urban public has become a feature of life which we ignore at our peril.

So it was that in 1983 I stopped formal census work at Wareham Forest, and it has never been reinstated. We replaced the formal census with a much simpler system which considered many of the same elements of information, but which estimated whether the population under review was rising or falling, expressed in simple percentage terms. Damage levels were reviewed, and at the end of this process, the previous year's proposed and actual cull figures were examined, to see if changes were necessary. The figures which were used in order to produce this assessment were those that the rangers had collected during the past year as part of their day-to-day activities, and so the information had cost very little to collate. The way we put together such an appraisal is now shown:

- We used information collected throughout the year, together with the stalker's judgement, to assess whether the population under review has increased, decreased or remained static during the past year. (If you prefer, the extent of the change can be expressed in percentage terms.)
- We related this assessment to known levels of deer damage, as well as known pressure on habitats, both to our own crops and to those of our neighbours or conservation sites.
- On this basis, we decided whether there was a need to modify the previous year's cull by increasing or decreasing it, and by what amount. (Again, percentages can be a useful way of approaching this task. If, for example, you consider that the population may have risen by 15 per cent, and if damage levels are still too high, you might decide to increase last year's cull by 25 per cent, and see whether that leads to improvements.) But you may simply decide that repeating last year's cull is the appropriate option.
- We assessed progress throughout the year, and revised our figures again the following year.

By using such an approach the information costs very little to collect, and the results are as good as anything else currently available. The important thing is that one is making identifiable assumptions, as well as moving forward from an established baseline and constantly reappraising your assumptions; and this becomes easier with time.

I asked Eric, and later Mark Warn and Vic Pardy, to help me to reappraise this approach at regular intervals, and we never saw evidence of worse deer management as a result. I would argue very strongly that the reverse was true. Free from the demand to produce meaningless figures, we began to concentrate upon improving our overall deer management package, to the extent that, in 1996, my last year with Forest Enterprise, we had put the whole operation into genuine profit – an achievement which I had always thought to be unattainable. I shall discuss how to look at the cost of deer operations in a balanced way and how to assess value for money in Chapter 6, but the Forest Enterprise, Dorset, example does illustrate what is possible on quite a large scale, given carefully targeted management and no compromise on standards.

I want to make it clear that I am not suggesting that attempts to count deer should automatically be stopped. Deer form part of a highly complex ecosystem, and blanket approaches cause more problems than they solve. An individual approach, depending on the local conditions, is what is required, and if census is thought desirable, for reasons which local managers can justify, then well and good. For most of us who are dealing with large areas and big populations or mixed species, as well as limited budgets, it is a luxury that we can manage without, with little or no detriment to the overall management. The important thing is to recognise that census work can be wasteful of time and money, and results are usually less than accurate. But if you feel that carrying out census work will aid your management then that is clearly a matter for you to decide. My purpose is to point out the pitfalls that are involved in building up a culling plan based on inaccurate data.

Alternatives to counting deer

It is one thing to be critical of past efforts to manage deer which are predominately based upon counting the population; it is quite another to suggest credible alternatives.

First it is necessary to have some idea of what is happening to any deer population, so that future work can be related to this estimate. This can be done simply by recording deer seen by reliable observers, together with details of where they were at the time, the configuration of the group and so on. Most stalkers find that they get an impression simply through carrying out these day-to-day observations as they go about their stalking. We have already agreed that such figures will give no more than a rough idea, but gathering them costs nothing, and it is better than having no information. What you get after a while is an impression of change. If, for example, you usually see fifteen or twenty deer on your stalking circuit and suddenly you find thirty-five you should start looking for an explanation. There may be an obvious cause such as an influx of deer because the neighbouring estate has been shooting pheasants, or there may be a more obscure reason. In the case of fallow or red deer, they could simply have come into your area as part of their cycle of movement across their home range; and they might just as easily be gone next day. It is always useful to learn how deer are using your land – do they live there all of the time, is their main base there, or are they regular or occasional visitors? There may be different combinations, particularly if more than one species are present. There could be many reasons for a sudden build-up, and you need to

'. . . and suddenly you find . . .' (RM)

look at each and eliminate them one by one until you are left with a likely cause, then keep it under review.

You also need to analyse the known deaths in the population during the last year. You should have records which will tell you this; but include known road casualties and poached deer as 'other deaths'.

At the end of this exercise you will have some idea of known changes to the population – that is all. You can, if you wish, build in information about likely reproductive rates, but I find that this does not help much. I look at how many deer were known to have died the previous year, and relate that to damage and complaints. I can then decide whether the current culling level should remain as it is or be increased or decreased. By what amount it should be altered is largely guesswork backed up by experience, and constantly fine-tuned in the light of new knowledge.

Be wary of sightings of deer reported by others, particularly in situations such as on shooting days. The farmer, as he goes about his daily business, will often have very useful information, particularly if he has an interest in deer, but counts on shooting days often fluctuate wildly. I can illustrate that with an example from the winter of 1995/6 from one estate where I manage the deer and also pick up on the game shoot.

Everybody on the shoot knows that Alan and I look after the deer, and there is always a bit of banter on shooting days. 'Deer are building up this year' is the usual opener. Even after all these years my inner reaction is always panic, though I try not to show it. Have I made a major error of judgement? Has something happened which we have not accounted for? Is the delicate balance of this system about to be upset? 'Saw thirteen today – all out of the Big Wood', the conversation continued, 'Deer all over the common', 'Five went out of Hanger Wood', and so on.

It is putting your finger on exactly what is happening that is the difficult bit. Several people told me over lunch of the deer they had seen during the day, and it all seemed to add up to more than the usual residents. During the afternoon, on the very last drive, I was placed near the shoot boundary. I did not get a shot, but I did have fourteen roe come back past me in three separate groups. I am sure that they were different animals, and I was not counting the same ones twice. A study of the estate map suggested the answer. When I traced the progression of the drives throughout the day I am sure that most if not all of the resident deer in the main wood were pushed across onto the neighbouring common during the morning. The last drive was across the common – effectively pushing the deer back again. I am sure that the number I saw arose from that combination of circumstances, and did not indicate a major build-up of numbers. Observations whilst completing the doe cull in February tended to confirm this view.

During the same winter, we encountered a similar problem. At the start of the winter I was recording 'few deer were seen', in my diary, the average we saw on our culling outings being seven. We shot four during this period, and I was concerned that this may have been too many. I need not have worried.

The winter cull at the end of February was slightly lower than usual, but during March large numbers of deer were being seen. It was common to count up to fifteen on a single field. This area does not normally suffer from the 'early bite syndrome' (see below). On 13 April we counted thirty-one different deer without covering more than about one third of the area.

Although our long-held views on the overall size of the population were severely tested by this, we remained convinced that there had not been an increase in the local population. Our level of culling should have prevented that. It was our guess that the long and unusual spell of north and north-east winds during the late winter had forced the deer normally resident on the open fields and hedges of the neighbouring estate to come into our area to find better shelter. It sounded a bit lame at the time to suggest that things would return to normal as the weather warmed up, but that is exactly what happened, and this winter the pattern was not repeated.

The spring bite phenomenon

By spring the deer will have survived the rigours of winter, and the females will need good nourishment to sustain the developing young they are carrying. For some time food will have been scarce, and even if it has been available in bulk the nutritional content will have been low. They desperately need plenty of food with high nutritional content but it is simply not available. Roe bucks will be growing their new antlers, and the males of the herd deer (red, sika and fallow) will almost certainly not have managed to recover body weight and condition following the autumn rut. So all deer will be hungry at this vital time, and many people find it hard to believe that often the most critical month is March, particularly when the weather has been severe and spring plant growth is late in starting. It is precisely because the deer are at a low ebb after surviving the rigours of winter that a delay in spring growth can lead to deaths from starvation. It is why the critical factor in determining the size of a deer population under natural conditions is the winter carrying capacity of the land. As is evident from articles written almost every year about Scotland, when deer populations on the hill are higher than the land can support, the result is often death from starvation. Whilst this is much rarer in the south it is by no means unknown, but I have found that in a population kept at artificially low levels in order to ensure woodland viability, winter deaths from starvation, or severe crop or tree damage are rare.

Bearing this in mind, I could sit down with an Ordnance Survey map each February and predict, with a fair degree of accuracy, where to expect complaints about deer damage during the coming few weeks. There are 'hot spots', usually a sheltered field or two, where, because of the shelter and aspect, plant growth begins early. Usually these are the same fields year after year, unless there are abnormal weather conditions. In this area most of the hot spots would be sheltered from the prevailing south-westerlies, and often surrounded by woodland. Growth may be up to three weeks earlier than in adjacent but more exposed fields.

The local farmer, looking out of his farmhouse window, may see twenty or thirty deer on his new ley day after day, and he wants to know what is to be done about it. Knowledge of the local situation now becomes very important. It is critical for the deer manager to be able to judge whether there is a genuine build-up, or whether it is simply that all of the deer in that area are coming to the only available, early food source after the winter's deprivation. When the deer population is carefully managed and the numbers are fairly low, the answer is most likely that they are coming to an early food source. If this is the case then as growth begins in other fields the deer will gradually disperse until things are back to normal, usually within two or three weeks.

Ashmore Dorset A History of the Parish

In Ashmore parish 1,723 poles of deer fence, five feet high, had to be kept up round the cultivated land, the only part of the parish from which the deer might be excluded, except from the copses less than three years old. A man still living has shot a stag by moonlight as it stood in the village street, from his bedroom window. Poaching, till the extinction of the chase rights in 1830, was hardly regarded as a crime.

In the daytime the deer would feed without fear among the sheep on the open downs. They were far too numerous and in a hard winter perished by thousands. In West Walk alone 500 young deer died in the winter of 1825 and the offence was such that the woodmen could not go to their work.

E. W. Watson MA

This extract was kindly provided by Mr E. Bourke of the Chettle Estate, Cranborne Chase, Dorset.

A sheltered combe where growth is at least two weeks earlier than nearby. (RM)

Having confidence in past deer management is the woodland manager's best asset in these situations, and although the farmer may not always be satisfied, there is little that can be done except to try and allay his fears. I can cite an example which is typical of this 'early bite syndrome', from an FC wood in central Dorset. This woodland straggles along the steep slopes of the chalk hills and totals some 800 acres (330 hectares) of forest which has been planted on former downland, rising to around 800 feet (250 metres) above sea level. The valleys are deep and rounded and the woodland and farmland form an intricate mixture. During most of the year the resident roe deer can be seen feeding in small groups, scattered around the woodland and field edges. Almost every year, as March approaches, groups of up to thirty can be found in a couple of fields which are in a sheltered combe, and where growth is usually at least two weeks earlier than anywhere else in this block. Every year it seems as though numbers have built up drastically, but before the end of the month those deer will have dispersed, and all will be back to normal. What happens is that most of the deer which live across this 1,200 acres or so of woodland and farmland will come to this one early food source as soon as the fresh growth begins – and who can blame them? Furthermore, this phenomenon invariably occurs during early March, when the females are protected by their close season, and when special dispensation would be required by law if crop damage was severe enough to justify shooting them out of season.

Many stalkers will be able to locate these 'early bite' areas, and I always try and explain to the farmer what is causing the temporary problem. If the farmer sees that the stalker is doing good work, the explanation will usually be accepted.

I can remember one area in Devon where the early bite often occurred on the forest firebreaks which bordered the major dual carriageways which bisected the forest, and there was often a rise in road deaths at this time of year.

Checking deer movements

March is also a time where a few evenings spent on a vantage point with a pair of binoculars will give a good idea of the deer which are around at that time. This is quite different from trying to assess the population; it is simply recording information about the habits of the deer on your management area, and the information will only tell you the situation on that particular evening. For example, one evening at the end of February 1997, Stuart Venables and I were looking for a final couple of sika hinds to complete our planned cull. We found forty-five in three fields. One was a mixed group, one a stag group and one a hind group. Three evenings previously I had toured the whole of the estate and found only three roe. It shows how quickly things can change as deer respond to the sudden growth of food plants.

A few evenings spent with binoculars are rarely wasted. (RM)

Making a new highseat. (RM)

Using a highseat. (RM)

Highseats

I like to visit all of my highseats during March, and check their condition to see if repairs, replacements, vegetation control or removal are necessary.

Highseats come in many designs, but the essential requirement is that they are safe to use. I have seen some which I would hesitate to use for firewood, and how nobody has fallen through or from them is a mystery. I will cheerfully use second-hand materials but they must be up to the job. I like to secure the rungs on wooden seats with fencing wire as well as nails, and although I have used nails to secure a seat to a shrub such as a holly, for example, which is of little value as timber, I would only do so if there is no feasible alternative.

Seats which rest against trees should be designed to allow fixing without nails. Modern designs invariably require tying with a length of rope, often using a fixing knot such as a Spanish windlass to apply tension to the rope. This is done by taking a fairly taut loop around the tree and the seat, then tensioning the rope by using a wooden bar which is inserted through the loop and twisted to take up any slack. The bar is then secured to the main rope to prevent the knot working loose.

In areas where seats have a tendency to 'disappear', it may be sensible to secure them to the trees with chains and locks.

Stalking paths

Cutting stalking paths is another spring job. I do very little of this, for several good reasons, but where it is required spring is a good time to get it done. A cleared path about 3 feet (1 metre) wide allows quiet access to a highseat or a secluded clearing, and this can make all the difference between success and failure, particularly when using highseats for morning stalks. When using them during the evening it is common to approach it at least an hour before dark, often longer. The deer may not be in the area, and even if they are and you disturb them, there is always a chance that they will settle down again whilst it is still light enough for you to operate. But at dawn the reverse applies. The approach is invariably made in the dark, and

A cleared path which allows access to quiet spots. (RM)

needs to be made very quietly, and the deer may be in the vicinity of the seat itself. Furthermore, at dusk the deer are often hungry and perhaps slightly more likely to take a chance. If they are disturbed at dawn, they usually flee to cover and just disappear.

I use few stalking paths largely because I do not have the resources to create and maintain them, and also because over the years I have got used to taking things as I find them. Alan and I both prefer to stalk on foot, so we try and use seats as little as possible. Where we do use them, we tend to restrict their use to evenings. I would think that less than 30 per cent of our deer are shot from seats. On the other hand, where seats are needed they are an indispensable aid to good deer management.

The greater safety of shooting from highseats becomes ever more important as public access increases, regardless of whether the land which you stalk is private or public. I have regularly found walkers who are a long way away from the nearest public right of way and who, when challenged, simply claim to be lost. It is never safe to assume that because land is private, no unauthorised walker will be using it. This reinforces the point that no stalker must ever shoot unless he is sure of a safe background. *If there is the slightest doubt about this – do not fire.*

Sometimes it is useful to have a clear path which allows quiet access to a favourite deer area. Hot spots are not restricted to early spring feeding areas; most areas which hold deer have favourite spots where deer may be found more often than not. These areas often provide seclusion, cover, shelter and food, and most stalkers get to know them as their knowledge of their area increases. Being able to approach such spots quietly and unobtrusively will often lead to success, and sometimes a stalking path is the simplest way of achieving this.

Crossing fences

Providing crossing places in fences, particularly barbed wire ones, can make a great difference, not only to your stalking, but also to your comfort. If you have left bits of yourself attached to rusty barbs in the past, you will know exactly what I mean; if not, may you be spared that experience. If you are like Alan, and stand 6 feet 6 inches, you may find that you take the average cattle fence in your stride, but I prefer to wrap the top wire with an old fertiliser sack, or a length of polythene hose or something similar, and secure it with baler cord or insulating tape.

No doubt the Health and Safety Executive will have a view on this, and I will be told that entry to all land must be through the approved entrance (the gate?), but deer stalking does not work that way. You have to approach deer where they happen to be feeding, and you do this by taking the wind into account, and also trying to remain unnoticed for as long as possible, which frequently means crossing obstacles such as wire fences. I therefore provide fence crossing places at regularly used spots, and pray avidly at less well used ones. Whilst on the subject of crossing obstacles, I hope you will always remember to make your weapon safe before tackling the obstacle.

Annual reports

Another job for spring is the completion of annual reports. These are an essential part of my deer work. In them I can report on progress during the previous year. I have always compiled annual reports, and I cannot now remember whether my original motivation was to provide information for the landowners for whom I have stalked or for myself – probably both. When I started doing this it was more or less unheard of except by one or two of the Deer Control Groups, but I am glad to see that this is slowly changing. Certainly I have always felt that if a landowner entrusts you with the privilege of managing deer on his land, the least you can do is provide a regular report setting out what has happened. Providing a report does not, of course, obviate the need for regular communication throughout the year, but it does provide a permanent record of progress. When I look back, mine provide a source of information and a real statement of progress over time. I did them at six-monthly intervals for many years, for no particular reason, but as my work increased I made it an annual report, which now goes to each landowner with the venison cheque. The information can be put together from your stalking diaries (I hope you keep stalking diaries!) and from your venison sales records. My reports include a brief resumé of what we were trying to achieve during the year, what we succeeded in achieving, a statement of accounts, a suggested plan for the next year, and anything else of interest which has occurred.

I always present my assessment of culling needs for the coming year together with my reasons for making these suggestions, but the final decision is taken by the owner. I am very conscious that I act as the 'servant' of the landowner, and that the final decision must be his. In fact I have never, in all the years I have operated this system, had an owner disagree substantially with my proposals, and only occasionally with even minor points, but I consider it extremely important to offer the option. Since this system runs year in, year out without any modification, it must have something to commend it.

It was my proud boast, until two years ago, that I had never lost a stalking area, so landowners must have liked the service Alan and I were providing. However, two years ago I did lose an area, and the way it happened provides a useful lesson. I had carried out deer control on a smallish mixed estate, and shot a few roe each year in order to protect the young trees. After we had reduced the population to a much lower level the need for regular visits became less, and the job became simply a 'watching brief'. This coincided with a time when I was under great pressure at work, and with family commitments; and I have to say that I neglected to communicate adequately with the owner. Finally he found someone else to do the work, and it was entirely my fault. So do keep on communicating – owners like to know what is going on, even though they might not always ask outright. Whilst this book has been in preparation, I have been asked to take on the woodland management of this small estate by the new owner – so things have, in one sense, come full circle. Perhaps I am forgiven.

Starting the roe buck cull

As April progresses and the days become longer, it is a good time to be out and about checking on your deer.

Roe bucks will be cleaning their newly grown antlers. Many older ones will be partially clean during the first few days of April, particularly in the south of Britain and especially if the weather has been warm. Cold weather seems to delay the cycle somewhat, and it may also be later further north. The older bucks clean first, and it is noticeable that some years seem to produce a crop of 'ragged' bucks, when the velvet seems to cling in tatters, whilst in other years the cleaning process passes much more neatly and most bucks appear fully clean.

The annual coat change

All deer will be changing from their winter to their summer coats, and this process invariably leaves then looking extremely ragged and motheaten. Roe seem to be worst in this respect as the old, thick winter coat falls out in handfuls. The transition from the heavy winter coat to the sleek, foxy red summer one is striking, and the new coat shows first on the neck and shoulders, and often along the flanks as well; with the rump and back the last to change. It is not uncommon for coat changing to continue well into June, and weather seems to be the main factor, with unusually warm and mild weather bringing about a quicker coat change.

The herd deer also change coat at this time of year and I have found that it is often the younger animals which appear in their full summer coat first. With red, fallow and sika the males are shedding their old antlers and beginning to grow the new ones. Antler growth in all deer is controlled by the annual rise and fall of the male sex hormone, testosterone, the old antlers being cast at the point in the cycle when the testosterone level is at its lowest. New antler growth begins immediately until, as the testosterone level peaks, growth ceases, the antlers are cleaned and the male is in breeding condition. The time of year varies from species to species, and April is particularly interesting because as the herd deer are casting their antlers, so roe bucks are cleaning theirs.

It always amuses me to watch a group of sika stags or fallow bucks during late March or early April, when some will have cast and others not. Some will be left with one antler for a day or so, and they really appear to be puzzled by this, wandering around shaking their heads in apparent disbelief at the uneven weight distribution. I have never been able to identify a constant pattern of antler casting in sika. Prickets sometimes cast before the big stags and sometimes after. Whilst roe bucks are becoming highly territorial at this time, male red, fallow and sika deer are preparing to live in all-male groups during the summer, until their new antler growth is complete.

Deer living in groups

Females tend to live in established groups throughout the year, and while fallow and red groups are quite large, this is not true of sika and roe. The normal female group of roe in spring usually consists of the mature doe, her doe yearling from two years before and any surviving kids from the previous year. Sika live in similar groups, the typical one being a trio of hind, yearling and calf. Where large groups of deer are seen together, it is normally in response to a particular food source, and they will consist of several smaller family groups. Normally they will split into their family units when they get back into cover again.

So early spring is a good time to check what is going on, to see where the deer are feeding on the 'early bite', and to watch as they disperse again for their summer cycle. You can get a good idea of where your roe bucks are, and of their quality, and this is a good time to shoot any surplus young bucks, whilst they are easily visible. As the new leaf growth comes through on the trees and shrubs in your woods, visibility decreases considerably, and that will become an important factor for the stalker as summer begins.

3.
SUMMER FOR THE WOODLAND DEER MANAGER

As spring slips into summer and the daylight hours increase further, the lowland deer manager approaches one of the most enjoyable yet physically most tiring times of the year. From May to mid-August is the peak period for the roe buck stalking season. Although they may legally be shot at any time from 1 April until 31 October, most stalkers concentrate on certain key periods as most interesting and potentially productive.

The roe buck cull

How surplus bucks are removed from the population will depend on your management objectives. There will be a fundamental difference in how you go about this task, depending on whether you are managing your deer with sport or woodlands as the primary objective.

If the provision of trophies is your main aim, you are most likely to be providing them for others rather than for yourself, usually for fee-paying recreational hunters. I have already discussed how, as a result of the very high rents they have to pay, many stalking tenants are forced to provide trophies for fee-paying clients. This is simply the only way in which they can recoup their outlay and expenses and make a living. We have also seen how many recreational hunters tend to influence the deer management system as a direct result of being customers who purchase stalking and bring substantial funds into the system. Stalking tenants who lease stalking for their own use are usually motivated by a similar desire to take high-quality trophies and again a primary consideration will be to get value for money. This can take the form of good trophies, plenty of shooting opportunities or both.

There are doubtless a few stalking tenants who are really interested in the kind of deer management which will minimise tree or crop damage, but they are rare and philanthropic individuals who, unless they find a knowledgable and sympathetic landlord, will pay handsomely for the privilege of doing someone else's work.

Another complication is the issue of sub-letting. Most people with whom I have discussed this practice consider it to be a curse. One person rents stalking and subsequently sub-lets it to a third party, perhaps to recoup the rent, to make a profit or to get rid of a potential liability. The financial pressure increases, because a further charge has been imposed, and so the sub-lessee is usually forced to invite visiting hunters in, who then dictate the objectives of deer management to a service provider who has little alternative but to agree. These objectives may be very different from those envisaged by the estate owner or agent, or even by the original lessee. Unless contracts are watertight – and often, because of their relative complexity and a lack of understanding of deer management amongst land agents, they are not – all kinds of problems may occur, and the owner may be left with at best, an embarrassing situation, and at worst a disaster.

Recreational hunters, like stalkers, vary widely in their experience and expectations. Many, although they may not be in a position to take on an area and manage the deer themselves, are nevertheless very knowledgeable about deer. Continental hunters will have received mandatory training, and will always possess a high level of knowledge about deer, but the continental hunting philosophy may not always be what we require in Britain, particularly where viable small woodland management is important. British hunters typically range from absolute novices to the very experienced, but again, in my experience their knowledge will very rarely include an appreciation of woodland management requirements.

There is an increasing tendency for recreational hunters to lease stalking in their own right, cutting out the middleman, the professional stalker, in the process. And one thing that virtually all of those that I have met have in common is that they want to ensure that they get what they are paying for. Many are successful business or professional men who are not easily fooled. They will tell you tales of sharp practice in the deer world, and of friends and acquaintances who have been cheated and they want to ensure that this does not happen to them. They are therefore on their guard, and will be looking for evidence that the service they are purchasing – often at high cost – represents value for money.

What better illustration of value for money is there than seeing plenty of deer around? This will help allay his fears that he is simply being relieved of his money. The problem comes, of course, if the hunter gets involved in deer stalking on an estate where deer are being managed with woodland viability in mind, because seeing plenty of deer around represents the exact opposite of what the system is trying to achieve. So it is important – very important – to be clear about what the landowner is aiming for. In the current climate of market-driven stalking rents this will not be easy, but one of my aims in writing this book is to show that there are alternative ways of doing things if your current system is not providing what is needed.

If you are managing deer primarily for woodlands, and use recreational hunters merely to increase income, it may be wise to indicate to prospective hunters that whilst you will be aiming to provide high-quality stalking experiences, the client should not expect to see large numbers of deer. If your visitors are accompanied at all times then this can of course be explained less formally during actual outings. My experience suggests that if you are really providing quality experiences, your clients are likely to return, regardless of how many deer they see. It is this quality experience that so many clients are seeking, and that includes sharing your knowledge of other wildlife and the countryside generally, as well as providing friendly companionship.

April and early May will provide a window of opportunity to reduce the number of young roe bucks which are about. The perceived wisdom of twenty years ago

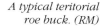

A typical teritorial roe buck. (RM)

was that one should keep territorial bucks because they would dominate the younger animals and keep their wilder instincts in check, including of course the desire to fray trees. This particular form of fraying resulted from territory marking rather than velvet cleaning. This idea of the 'unpaid policeman' had a lot of followers in the early 1970s, but I found that it simply did not work for me. If the population – in this instance the population of potential territorial males – was too high, then damage levels became unacceptable – it was as simple as that. As far as I could see the presence or absence of a local territorial buck made not the slightest difference to this basic principle. It may be in the interest of many deer managers to encourage and foster territorial males simply because these are the nucleus of the breeding population, but that decision should, in my opinion, be based on the quality of the individual, not simply because the male is territorial. For example, I would remove a lower-quality territorial buck from the population almost irrespective of other factors, and expect that the gap thus created would be filled by a better, younger animal. What is initially difficult for most deer managers is to recognise the point at which things become unacceptable and, following remedial action, the point at which they are again acceptable; and this brings us back to our aims of management.

I have tried various ways of manipulating roe buck populations, ranging from deliberately removing territorial or stand bucks to keeping them at all costs. If containing woodland deer damage is important to you, then the way to do it is to reduce the whole population to quite low levels and keep it there; and this is usually best achieved by weighting the buck cull towards younger bucks, of which there will usually be a surplus. I would incline towards keeping good stand bucks as the nucleus of the breeding stock, but this view probably has more to do with my own preferences than any logically defensible technique.

My personal preference is to remove most of the young males which are required during April and early May, whilst territories are not fully established, and whilst the woods have good visibility. Very old and unusual bucks should be shot at any time during the open season, unless there is a particular reason for sparing one; but most chances for them are likely to arise during the rut, in late July and August. This approach works well, regardless of whether you are involved with recreational hunters or not, and enables you to spread the key times in your work schedule.

Summer roe buck stalking is not a simple operation by any means, particularly if your system requires you to accommodate fee-paying recreational hunters. It

Unusual bucks should be shot at any time – a perruque roe buck, Dorset 1993. (RM)

becomes especially difficult if you are working to demanding targets but one consolation is that you are able to get out in the countryside in its spring and early summer glory.

I put forward my ideas about targets for the coming year's cull when I do my annual reports, at the end of the winter period, taking into account the following factors:

- the number of deer known to have died during the past year
- the levels of damage to forest, farm and horticultural crops during the last year, and the type of damage being experienced
- the stalker's assessment of whether the population is increasing or decreasing, and whether the population needs to be reduced or maintained at current levels
- the stalker's assessment of the annual reproductive rate of the population
- other information which may be relevant

The size of the buck cull will be decided in line with the management objectives, and at the same time I will make an assessment of whether achieving this plan is realistic, taking into account the time and resources available. In my view, culling sufficient male deer of any species, with the probable exception of muntjac, should not be a major problem for any serious stalker. The season is long, and males are generally easier to stalk – by a very big margin – than females. Furthermore, the best times of the year, from a climatic viewpoint, are available to the stalker. So the size of the male cull should not present a serious problem and selective culling becomes viable. I will discuss selective culling – or rather non-selective culling – in more detail when discussing the very important female cull in Chapter 5, but I have found from past experience that the degree of selection I am able to implement is actually quite limited.

As far as setting a figure is concerned, the first few years of a new management programme are the most difficult, as any figures used will be largely guesswork. However, you have to start somewhere, and if damage control is urgently required I would start by taking the owner's assessment of the deer population, together with any other local knowledge which may be available, and double that figure. I would assume that the male/female ratio is 1:1.5, and plan to cull 50 per cent of the population in the first full year. I would also plan to achieve a male/female cull ratio of at least 1:1.5; and 1:2 would be better. At the end of the year I will have a much better idea of what the situation is (although it will have changed of course), and also whether my original plan was seriously flawed.

If damage control is not an immediate issue I would plan to cull 35 per cent of the estimated population, and amend this in the light of future experience. The same male/female cull ratio of 1:1.5 or 1:2 would apply, even in this lower overall cull.

In my early days managing deer most experts advised trying to keep populations stable, and that is where they came into direct conflict with the forest industry, which often advocated extermination, or at the very least much lower numbers. Managing a population in order to steadily reduce the numbers was never really put forward as a serious option but I invariably found that keeping a stable population, assuming that you are able to tell when the population is stable, and for how long, was simply not acceptable if damage reduction was an objective. In almost all the deer populations that I have been involved in managing over the years, reducing numbers sooner or later became an overriding priority. I needed to find a way to minimise damage to woodlands, whilst also allowing deer to flourish, and I am satisfied that the answer lies in maintaining populations at a lower level than the habitat is able to support. It is then possible to have the best of both worlds: deer damage at acceptable levels and the deer seen as assets rather than as liabilities. Clearly, if the only, or main, motivation is to manage deer to provide sport then the objectives may be quite different, but if this option is chosen one cannot complain if damage, or the cost of preventing such damage reaches unacceptable levels.

When selecting the animals to be shot it also helps to have an estimation of age, and my next task is to look at that aspect. I have never met anybody who could, with accuracy and reliability, age wild deer in the field whilst they were still alive. It is quite difficult to be accurate even when they are dead; the most reliable method is by tooth sectioning which is rather time-consuming. The basic idea of age-structured culling is that if you do an accurate census of your deer population, and are able to say, for example, how many males you have in the current year's population, which are one-year-old, how many two-year-olds, how many three-year-olds and so on, you can then predict how many of each age class you need to shoot in order to keep the population stable, reduce it, or allow it to increase. However, I find it difficult to breathe life back into an animal once I have realised that I have shot one which does not accord with the age-structured pyramid plan, so adopting a system which depends upon selectively shooting male deer across a predetermined range of age classes seems to me to be doomed to failure. At the very least it results in turning down lots of shooting opportunities. However, most continental sportsmen take great pride in assessing their bucks and stags, so perhaps it comes back to whether your primary motivation is sport or deer management. I want a reasonably balanced deer population, regardless of species, which is kept artificially lower than the habitat is able to support. In that way my trees and neighbour's crops seem to do quite well, and I know that this approach will also encourage a vibrant and healthy deer population. In order to achieve this I have never been able to rely on the recommended principles of age-structured culling, which approach the matter from the angle of creating and maintaining a sporting resource, because these simply do not work when the stalker is working to woodland management targets.

The best I have ever been able to achieve in ageing deer in the field is to place them within the general categories of old, middle-aged and young. I can guess at more precise ages, probably as well as most stalkers, but we need rather more than guesswork if we are to build a sustainable system and I am always trying to find ways of reducing guesswork to its minimum. Although it is not an exact classification I can live with old, middle-aged and young, however, and find it quite reliable for roe, fallow, sika and red under normal field conditions. It is quick to assess in the field, and reduces mistakes to a minimum without, as far as I can see, causing any loss in the quality of management; and the same basic approach is also suitable for dealing with muntjac. The way in which the definitions are applied is important, however, so I will set out how I regard them (the ages given here refer to roe, and are for guidance rather than as a definitive statement):

- A young animal is not fully mature or developed, although it may be capable of breeding. It has a lightly boned body, with a short face, holds its neck high and is inquisitive. 0–2 years of age.
- A mature animal has a fully developed body, and is in prime breeding condition. It is the nucleus of any population. The body is solid, the face longish, and it is alert and cautious. 3–6 years of age.
- An old animal is past its physical prime and shows distinct signs of old age, although it may still be able to breed. It may suffer from arthritis or worn teeth, and finds it more difficult to survive. It has a heavy body, holds its neck low, and moves slowly. Over 6 years of age.

A middle-aged roe buck. (RM)

An old roe buck. (RM)

An ideal population for my woodland management objectives, would probably contain 10 per cent old animals (on the basis that it will usually be impossible to remove all of these from the stock), 45 per cent middle-aged animals and 45 per cent young animals which will mature and form replacements in due course. These figures would apply to both male and female populations.

Having decided on the roe buck cull for the summer period, you need to look at what else there is to do. That depends on what other species are being managed. My experience has been with roe as either the sole species or with fallow or sika, but as muntjac are forcing themselves more and more to the forefront of deer management in developing woodlands, and because of their unusual breeding cycle, they present a particular set of problems which require consideration.

Muntjac

Muntjac are small deer of Asiatic origin which breed continuously throughout the year. Fossil discoveries suggest that they have changed little since prehistoric times, and as Alan Lewis would undoubtedly say, 'If they've been around for that long they must be doing something right.' Although females have been recorded carrying twin foetuses, there seem to be few recorded instances of twin births; the usual pattern is for females to carry and rear a single kid. Thirty-six hours after the female gives birth she is usually mated again, whilst still heavily lactating. Most females are mated when they reach seven months, and give birth for the first time at fourteen months. There is no time during the year when muntjac females may be controlled

A muntjac buck.
(DS)

Muntjac can cause serious damage to native flora. (RM)

Bee orchid (Ophrys apifera)

Wild daffodil (Narcissus pseudonarcissus)

Cowslip (Primula veris)

without the possibility of leaving dependent young. The best that can be hoped for is that to minimise the chances of this happening, and even that is difficult and requires fine judgement. Young are born throughout the year but there seems to be a tendency towards more births during the period from March to September.

Young muntjac bucks grow their first set of antlers at around five months, regardless of when they are born. These antlers are cast during the June of the following year, when a new set begins to develop. The fully grown antlers are cleaned towards the end of August, and into September, but bucks are capable of mating during the period when the antlers are cast.

It is difficult to age muntjac successfully in the field but young animals tend towards thin necks and a rather 'juvenile' appearance, whilst mature animals have thicker bodies. Old animals tend to have short, thick necks, heavy bodies and sagging bellies. Young bucks have long pedicles (the bony growths from the skull which support the antlers), but these get shorter at each casting.

The muntjac stalker's job is therefore fraught with difficulties, particularly in situations where it is necessary to reduce numbers; and there is as yet no clear consensus on the best way to proceed. The law does not help, since there is no close season. There is little doubt at all that they are capable of building up populations very quickly, and that those populations, once established, are capable of causing severe and sustained damage to the native flora of ancient woodlands and conservation sites. Although males fray all kinds of herbage and some forest and woodland trees up to 2 inches (5 cm) in size, the effect on forest crops is rarely significant, but woodland damage also occurs through browsing. Furthermore, because muntjac are ideally suited to exploiting younger woodland crops, they often proliferate in young or semi-mature woods or young crops in older woodlands, where it becomes extremely difficult to locate them, let alone shoot enough to minimise the damage.

Many deer managers believe it is virtually impossible to prevent muntjac from establishing themselves in new areas, because by the time they are seen regularly a nucleus colony will already be established, and the chances of getting on top of the population are low unless the stalker is prepared to shoot on sight, regardless of humanitarian considerations.

Some deer managers have introduced their own standards for culling muntjac and I am indebted to Keith 'Brad' Bradbury, Chief Ranger with Forest Enterprise in East Anglia, for allowing me to publish his views on muntjac management as well as on best practice for culling females. I consider these guidelines to be the best that are currently available for managing these unusual deer under normal woodland conditions in the most humane way possible.

- Shoot males more or less indiscriminately at any time, unless you are trying to produce high-quality trophies, in which case shoot males with poor antlers only.
- Bucks tend to patrol their territories and can often be located at ride crossing spots, where they may present a shooting chance.
- Do not shoot slim females. Only shoot females when they are clearly pregnant. There is no other way of knowing whether the female in question is barren or has dependent young. *Shoot fat females.*
- If a female is with a male she may be ready to mate, and therefore with dependent (lactating) young nearby. Do not shoot unless there is a critical need.

It is clear from this that finding effective yet humane ways of managing muntjac in situations where populations need to be substantially reduced represents a real challenge. The rules of thumb given above represent a good first step towards meeting that challenge, but there is still much to learn.

Fallow, sika and red in summer

Summer presents the woodland deer manager with an opportunity to have a look at the male populations of other species in the area. Fallow and sika males like to get out of the woods during late summer in order, presumably, to escape the flies. They are often to be found in late summer crops such as corn fields, or in secluded grass fields carrying lush grass. During the summer of 1996, on one of the areas which I manage, a group of up to thirty-five sika stags were to be found day after day for three or four weeks in a quiet field where the farmer had not cut the hay. They did not do much damage on that occasion, but a similar sized group in a corn field could cause substantial damage. Normally at least as much damage is caused by the deer lying down and flattening the corn as by eating it. They often seem to eat much more of the little weeds which grow among the corn as they do of the corn itself, although when they are living in a grass field they do eat the fresh grass.

Late summer is a good time to get an idea of how many are about and where they are, although they may well disappear onto somebody else's land as the territorial urge becomes stronger and as they return to their traditional rutting habitat, ready to mate in due course. This process usually starts in early September, ready for the rut to peak in October. Male red, fallow, and to a rather lesser degree sika, can travel long distances during the summer, sometimes several miles. So summer populations are no guarantee of what may happen later in the year. However, it is a pleasant time to be out and about, and some useful information can be gathered.

Birth

Red, fallow, roe and sika females typically give birth during the last half of May and the first two weeks of June. Well over 90 per cent of births will take place during that period, although there can be wide individual variations. Muntjac exhibit a similar tendency, in that most births probably take place during the late spring and summer period, but as we have seen they can and do give birth at any time.

For roe the mating and pregnancy phase is rather unusual, whilst for red, sika and fallow it is, in a biological sense, straightforward and uncomplicated. Since the females of all four species give birth at the same time, and yet the mating time for roe is significantly different to the others, there must be an unusual factor at play,

A young roe kid, only a few days old. (RT)

and it takes the form of a process known as delayed implantation, a process which, to the best of my knowledge, roe have in common with badgers and seals. What it means is that the egg is fertilised at the time of mating (late July to early August), but it is not implanted into the uterine mucosa until some time in late December. Following implantation into the uterus, development proceeds normally until birth in May or June. Delayed implantation may be an evolutionary measure designed to avoid the effects of severe weather on heavily pregnant females.

Roe commonly give birth to twins whilst the herd deer usually have singletons. My own records for roe over a ten-year period on a Dorset estate show 77.5 per cent of pregnant females carrying twins and 22.5 per cent carrying singletons. None was found carrying three. I have only two confirmed records of roe does carrying three young, one of which was a doe killed in a road traffic accident near Wareham in Dorset in June 1986, just days before she would have given birth. I am unable to say with any certainty whether there is any relationship between the age of the pregnant female and the incidence of twins, although it is my impression that a higher proportion of singleton-bearing does are younger animals, possibly carrying their first kids. My records show that it is very unusual to find any doe over one year old which is not pregnant, and also that there is an exact distribution of the sexes among the young produced: 50 per cent male and 50 per cent female over many years, but with a wide seasonal variation in any given year. I have not seen an example of fallow, sika or red twins, although there are recorded examples from time to time. They represent a very tiny percentage of births however, certainly thousandths of a per cent, and for all practical purposes may be disregarded. In my Dorset roe population, 75 per cent of the single pregnancies which were recorded occurred during the first three years of the management programme, whilst no single pregnancy was recorded in four of the last seven years. I think this represents nature's way of compensating for the unexpected pressure on the population caused by the introduction of our management programme.

Young deer are totally dependent upon their mothers for some weeks after birth, with the level of dependence falling as the youngster takes more and more organic matter. Many young deer suckle up to twenty weeks or longer, but the balance of milk to vegetable food shifts markedly after ten weeks or so. Young deer will be seen taking edible morsels of tender green food from the age of three weeks, but gradually it becomes a larger and larger constituent of their diet, and eventually overrides their dependence on the lactating mother. Most young deer lose the 'baby' or spotted coat of their birth at around ten weeks of age.

One thing has become very clear to me over the years. The reproductive potential of all the deer populations which I have worked with has been more than adequate. I find it difficult to envisage any culling strategy which could be carried out using normally accepted ethical principles, which would put any of these populations under severe threat, and even if it did happen a reduction of culling pressure would soon redress the balance. However, that assumes a degree of sensitivity in the deer manager, and also assumes that the population is being managed for reasons other than financial overexploitation and is not unduly affected by external factors over which the deer manager has no control, such as poaching.

The roe rut

As July progresses most roe stalkers will be eagerly preparing for the rut, the period when mating takes place, and the basis is laid for a new generation. This is usually an enjoyable and rewarding period for the stalker but can also be quite a disappointment. I like to get the largest part of my roe buck cull out of the way long before the rut so that I can enjoy simply being out and about with the deer at this rather personal period in their lives, but if you are involved in client stalking you will certainly be looking for bucks to shoot during the rut.

Most mating activity will take place between 20 July and 12 August, certainly on my areas in the 'soft south'. I have seen roe mating on five occasions, four times (in different years) on 4 August and on the other occasion on the 5th. That signifies very little except perhaps coincidence, but I am certainly out and about on those dates each year, as long as the weather is reasonable. The August of 1996 was a case in point. On the 4th I reached my destination at around 4.45 a.m. and set off up the valley with my cameras. I spotted three deer which, as I got nearer, proved to be a buck and two does. The buck was very interested in one of the does, and was ignoring the other. The chosen doe was leading him quite a merry dance, round and round in circles and figures of eights, whilst the buck kept his nose as near to her rump as he possibly could. Finally they moved off into the wood, where doubtless mating eventually followed.

Later that morning whilst deeper in that same wood, I found another buck, again with a doe, and watched them for over an hour while they mated seven or eight

I watched them for an hour whilst they mated 7 or 8 times. (RM)

Unseasonal mating-type behaviour – roe, Dorset, April 1997. (RM)

times. I was within twenty yards of them for all of that time and managed to get a few photographs, but how I wished I were Alan; at 6 feet 6 inches (almost 2 metres) he would have been able to see above the bracken, whereas most of my shots were partially obscured by ground vegetation.

Calling roe during the rut is an experience never to be forgotten, and my mind goes back to the first buck I saw Bill Hendy call, in Devon many years ago. It was on the far side of a valley, about three hundred yards away, and at the call he came straight toward us until, after Bill had indicated that he could be taken, I shot him at twenty-five yards. On another evening in a nearby wood we had a buck under the legs of the Thetford highseat in response to Bill's call. Yet on other occasions bucks will take no notice at all of any efforts to call them, and I put this down to the fact that they are with a doe which is ready to mate and are not willing to give up a certainty on the off-chance of another opportunity. As Bill would doubtless say, 'Would you?'

This is a lovely time of year, and one to be enjoyed. If you are ever given the opportunity to go out with an experienced caller, walk over broken glass if necessary, but get there on time. You will learn a great deal about deer and their habits in a very short space of time. Sometimes when a buck will simply not respond to your doe call, you can try reproducing the distress call of a kid calling to its mother. This will result in the doe coming to the call, and often she will be followed by a buck which may be in attendance. Personally I do not like doing this, but it will sometimes bring an old buck, which you may otherwise have difficulty in getting. In fact, I do not like shooting deer during the rut, and rarely do so unless an old timer or a deformed animal turns up, but that is simply a personal preference. I do value the chance to get very close to wild deer, and this can often be better achieved during the rut than at any other time.

The drawbacks of summer stalking

If there is a more pleasurable pursuit for the deer manager than stalking a roe buck on a lovely summer evening then I have yet to find it. But that is only one side of the story. There are drawbacks, including the heat, flies and other biting insects, stinging nettles and other vicious plants and high, wet vegetation, and these plagues can test the resilience of the most dedicated stalker.

In addition, there are the hours. Every stalker has to work long hours and the antisocial aspects of the job are often swept under the carpet. But they can cause considerable domestic distress. In summer the hours are much worse, tied as they are to the key daily stalking peaks around dawn and dusk. For the sport stalker this time can usually be fitted in with other arrangements, but the professional who takes out recreational hunters as part of his living has more of a problem. During the summer it will be normal to be up at 3.30 a.m., often not getting back to bed until nearly midnight. Try that for a week, and by the end you will be acutely aware of the problem. A stalker will have done four hour's work before most people start their working day, and will be doing at least another four or five in the evening. On top of that he has to boil out heads for his recreational hunters, and work on Saturday and often Sunday to complete his bookwork for the week and see his clients off. When I became aware of how physically and mentally demanding this period was, I made it an unwritten rule that each Forestry Commission ranger under my jurisdiction would have one week free of recreational hunters after each full week of client stalking. It was another of my rules that every recreational hunter was always accompanied by a ranger, not simply taken to a highseat, dumped for three hours and then collected again.

Another problem is keeping dry. Surprising as it may seem, I get wetter stalking in summer than I do in winter, at least on morning stalks, because the vegetation is so much higher. If you have ever tried to creep around the edge of a summer cornfield before the corn has been cut, or along an unmown woodland ride from mid-May onwards, you will know that you are likely to find at least 3 feet (1 metre) of lush growth, all dripping from the overnight dew. It matters not whether you walk tram lines or the headland, you will still be soaked, if not from the corn then from the mass of other summer herbage which borders the field. I have never quite managed to come to terms with the fact that I am more likely to get my legs and lower body wet on an early summer morning than when stalking in winter so that I usually forget to take waterproof overtrousers. I still look up at a clear blue sky and think 'Oh, no need for waterproofs today', and I still finish many stalks regretting my decision. The dew is transferred to your body up to at least waist height, and your clothing acts like a wick. During winter it is unusual to have to travel through vegetation higher than, say, calf height when actually stalking.

In addition to moisture, some people seem to attract all manner of crawling and biting things, and suffer much more than others from the resulting bites and stings. And Murphy's law dictates that you will be attacked at the least convenient moment. You will have been sitting for an hour waiting for a deer to show, and just as the buck appears you become aware of a quiet buzz around the back of your neck. You ignore it, but it will not go away. It flies under your nose and around your ears, and gets tangled in your eyelash, and finally you decide that the only option is to swat it, whereupon, the 'scout' is immediately joined by the main infantry. You will be lucky if the buck fails to spot your frantic arm and hand movements as you try to repel the attackers.

This, I am afraid, is part and parcel of summer stalking, and the attackers come in many forms, from various biting flies, to clegs, horseflies, gnats, mosquitos and wasps. All seem to bite or sting and I really admire those phlegmatic individuals who can simply grin and bear it. I cannot, and so I have to resort to some form of insect protection. Some people suffer quite badly from the effects of stings and bites, and if you are really susceptible, then summer stalking may not be the best way to spend your time. I come up in various lumps, but have become hardened to them over the years. However, it is the irritating effect of buzzing insects which annoys me. I do use insect repellant, and various proprietary brands seem quite successful. My personal favourite is Jungle Formula, but others seem to be equally effective. You need to use fairly liberal applications and to follow the instructions on the label. Most need to be applied to exposed skin, and it never hurts to apply some to your hat, collar and cuffs as well. This does not do a lot for your sex appeal, but you are, after all, stalking deer. After a while your stalking clothes show dark patches where the repellant has been regularly applied, but the effects can normally be minimised by a quick immersion in the washing machine.

There are two more particular insect-based problems which the woodland stalker may well come across, and neither is very pleasant. They are ticks and Lyme disease, and they are closely connected. The tick which causes the problem is the sheep tick (*Ixodes ricinus*). Its animal hosts include deer, foxes, squirrels, mice and other rodents, as well as sheep, and it is easily transmitted to dogs. Dorset seems to have very high tick levels. When I moved to Dorset I noticed that I was finding many more ticks on my dogs in spring and summer than had been the case in Devon. It soon became obvious that culled deer were also carrying many more ticks; in fact most Dorset deer, either from the chalk uplands or from the acid heathlands, are heavily laden with ticks, irrespective of body condition, although weak or injured animals seem to be particularly affected.

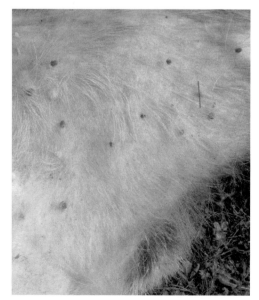

Dorset is a county with very high tick levels. (RM)

It is quite common for deer stalkers to get tick bites – indeed it can happen to anyone who walks in the countryside in tick-infested areas. Over the years I have learned to recognise tick bites by the particular itch they cause, and although this does not sound very scientific it works. There is a peculiar quality to the itch of a tick bite. Ticks crawl onto your clothing as you brush against vegetation, or when you are handling shot deer; it is very difficult to prevent this happening unless you are prepared to wear full protective clothing at all times. Various suggestions are made, such as tucking your trousers into your socks, wearing long trousers, using repellants on your clothing, brushing off your clothing before entering your house and checking your body for ticks. All are sound, common-sense precautions which should be followed, but I find that all the stalkers that I know get tick bites on a regular basis in spite of taking these steps.

Ticks are really quite unpleasant, and tend to attach themselves in the most inconvenient places. They feed by penetrating the skin and sucking blood, and they then drop off unaided after gorging for several days, by which time they have grown from the size of a coarse crystal of sugar to the size of a garden pea. Favourite lodging places seem to be around the waistband of the trousers, in the groin, behind the knee joint, and even on the scrotum.

When I find one that has embedded its feeding tube in my skin, I usually manage to dislodge it by grasping the tick carefully, as close to its head as possible, with tweezers. Other methods include immersing it in surgical spirit until it lets go, or touching it with a lighted cigarette end. You could, of course, immerse the tick in alcohol before using tweezers on it, to make doubly sure. You need to avoid leaving the head under the skin, since this can set up a nasty secondary infection, and so, clearly, a period of immersion prior to removing it could help to prevent this.

Most tick bites simply cause a small red rash for a day or two and an irritating itch, but some ticks can transmit Lyme disease, and that is a different matter altogether.

Lyme disease is named after a small town in the USA where it was first discovered in 1975. Cases began to appear in Britain during the mid-1980s. It is really quite nasty, and all that I can do here is to alert you to the symptoms and advise you to seek medical advice without delay. However, since many doctors are still unfamiliar with the disease, they may not specifically look for it.

Lyme disease is a bacterial infection carried by the tick, which is transmitted to humans as a result of a bite. As I understand it the combination of circumstances for a human to be infected are that the tick must be carrying the bacteria and the person who is bitten must be susceptible to the disease. Since only a small proportion of ticks may be carrying the bacteria and not everyone is susceptible, the chances of getting the disease are somewhat reduced. Nevertheless, although it is entirely treatable if it is recognised and treated early, it can be very unpleasant, and can cause serious long-term health problems. So recognising the symptoms and getting proper medical attention is vital. It is also wise to assume that any tick bite can lead to Lyme disease, and to monitor the bites accordingly. It is believed that if an infected tick is removed within twenty-four hours of embedding, the risk of infection is reduced, but it is always wise to save any tick which you have removed from your skin in a sealed container, in case you develop symptoms later. The most obvious symptoms are:

- The first sign is usually a red rash around the bite site, which starts a few days after being bitten and often begins as a red spot. This enlarges, usually as a faint pink ring with a clear centre, or it may be barely noticeable.
- This is often accompanied by flu-like symptoms or chills, which may be coupled with headaches, tiredness or aching joints. At this stage the disease responds well to treatment with antibiotics, but if left untreated various complications may occur which may lead to long-term health problems with arthritic, neurological or cardiac origins.
- Fever is more common in children.

Any tick bite which seems in any way out of the ordinary should be investigated immediately by seeking proper medical advice. And do ensure that your doctor knows that you suspect Lyme disease so that the appropriate tests can be carried out quickly.

It is not only insects that can hurt you. There are various plants which do their best to ruin your stalking. Brambles, nettles, thorns, even dry bracken stalks present various hazards, whilst your poor dog, particularly if it is a long-haired breed such as a spaniel, not only picks up ticks in profusion, but also burdock heads, thistle heads and all sorts of other things which require attention with a wire comb.

By the time you have been bitten and stung, and have run the risk of cutting yourself on bracken stalks, you may reach the conclusion that it would have been easier and less painful to have stayed at home. But if none of this succeeds in putting you off, you will probably make a stalker!

Deer damage

Deer damage can occur at any time of year, but damage to certain farm crops takes place in summer, so it is best to look at it here. It can be caused in several ways, usually as a result of one or more of the following activities:

- fraying in order to clean velvet from growing antlers
- fraying in order to mark territories
- stripping bark from trees
- scoring the boles of trees
- browsing trees, shrubs, ground flora and coppice regrowth
- grazing agricultural or horticultural crops
- trampling or rolling on agricultural crops

Fraying can be caused by any species of deer, except Chinese water deer, which have no antlers, but

Fraying velvet on a young pine tree. (RM)

A fallow buck marking his territory – using a fallen fir tree. (RM)

Bole scoring by sika – in this case on laurel. (RM)

Browsing damage to native shrubs. (RM)

fraying damage by muntjac is much less likely to be economically significant. Fraying is most apparent on crop trees, often along plantation edges or rides. The effect can be minimised by removing surplus young males from the population and by leaving alternative fraying stocks, such as coppice stools or unwanted trees. Fraying usually kills or totally distorts the target tree, thus greatly reducing or eliminating its timber value.

Whenever the male population is too high, undue competition results, and excessive fraying is done to mark territories. The best approach is again to reduce the number of surplus young males, and if damage is still too high remove some of the territorial males as well. This damage tends to be most common with fallow and roe and like fraying to remove velvet, it invariably ruins the target tree.

The stripping of bark is most common amongst herd deer, and it is thought to be caused by deer searching for minerals in the cambial layers, often during the winter period. Sika and red are the main offenders, but fallow will also strip bark at times. It can affect trees up to 8 inches (20 cm) in diameter, and will often reduce the value of the tree substantially. It is important not to confuse this with damage caused by grey squirrels or rabbits. .

Bole scoring is done mainly by sika, and the reason is not fully understood. It may be due to stress or frustration, and this, in turn, may be due to an excessive male population. Deep gouges are made in the bark of semi-mature trees, even on shrubs such as laurel. The tree may survive but its growth rate and value will be substantially reduced.

Deer eat vegetation. If the plant which is eaten is being grown as a crop, then the deer is brought into conflict with the farmer or the forester. If it is being nurtured on a conservation site, then the deer is brought into conflict with the conservationist. Browsing the leading shoot off a branch forces the tree or shrub to respond by growing from lateral buds, which results in distortion. At its most severe, browsing pressure prevents seedling trees or coppice regrowth from surviving. Tree distortion is important when growing trees to produce timber, but severe browsing can cause unacceptable damage to vegetation on conservation sites as well. Severe browsing damage is usually caused when a deer population is too high to allow sufficient woodland regeneration, although the population may not be too high for sporting objectives. Occasionally it may simply be that the area subjected to browsing is a 'hot spot', and preventative measures such as fencing or tree protection may be necessary.

When the vegetation being grazed is an agricultural or horticultural crop, the reasons for concern are obvious. But similar damage may have been caused by other animals and it is vital to take this into account and differentiate deer damage from that caused by sheep, rabbits or hares, whether it is browsing or grazing damage.

Trampling or rolling is not normally a problem in woodlands, although evidence of bedding-down spots is often apparent. It may become a problem on small conservation sites, but it is most common in agricultural crops such as corn, and in some instances it can affect the yield.

These are the main types of damage caused by deer, but there are one or two situations where deer can cause quite severe damage, such as in root crops like turnips or mangolds. Here the damage can be quite severe for a rather unusual reason. Deer have no upper incisors, so in order to secure food they need to grip the item by squeezing it between the lower incisors and the upper hard gum. The deer then flicks its head to break it off. When a deer flicks a young tree, the tree severs at the point of grip, but with root crops such as turnips, particularly when they have been planted in shallow or light soils, the flick often pulls the plant out of the ground. Sometimes the deer manages to take a mouthful, but sometimes the plant is simply discarded, with only the tooth marks giving a clue to the cause. In order to get another mouthful the deer is then forced to move on to another plant, often with similar results. It takes little effort to imagine the result of, say, a herd of red deer visiting a root field in hard weather over a period of several nights – the crop can be devastated. However, I have often found roe feeding on stubble turnips in severe weather and not dislodging them at all. The deer will then feed much more on a single plant, and much less overall damage will be done. The scale of the problems often depends on how long the severe weather lasts.

Incidentally the habit of flicking makes it easier to identify young trees browsed by deer; the cut is distinctly ragged, unlike that of, say, a rabbit or a hare, where the cut is sharp and clean.

Another crop which can cause particular problems for the deer manager is maize. A relatively new introduction to Britain, it is spreading in its use and in the acreage grown. Maize provides security, shelter and food for deer of all species for nearly the whole of its growing period, because it grows tall and dense and is not harvested until early autumn. It commonly grows up to 5 feet 6 inches (1.75 metres), and as high as 6 feet 6 inches (2 metres) on some soils. As far as I am aware no other agricultural crop in common use provides as many advantages for deer, and they are not slow to exploit this opportunity. Once they have found some maize, they are extremely difficult to dislodge from it, irrespective of the size of the population. The problem is particularly acute where maize fields border or are near to attractive lying-up cover. It therefore provides an unusual problem for the deer manager, and the problem is growing as the amount of maize being planted continues to increase. Serious deer damage is usually traceable to one of two factors: either the resident population is too high or there is a hot spot where deer congregate, and where damage will occur irrespective of the size of the population. In agricultural crops, damage often ocurrs when abnormally large numbers of deer (usually of the larger species – red, fallow and sika) visit a particular crop at a certain time in order to exploit a short-term situation. The resident population is increased by visiting deer which come to this particular food source.

Many crops provide such hot spots, but the deer usually disperse to their normal locations quite rapidly, and so the problem is usually relatively short-term, although if large numbers of deer, particularly herd deer, visit a field, even if it is only for a few days, substantial damage can be caused. However, many farmers with whom I have discussed this problem are of the opinion that if the overall population is reasonably low, such damage is usually overcome as the crop puts on bulk and volume. Again there seems a compelling case for managing deer to keep their overall numbers reasonably low, as both agricultural and woodland damage are then usually kept to acceptable levels.

The situation with maize is very different, however, and causes considerable concern both to farmers and deer managers. My experience suggests that preventing deer damage or keeping it to acceptable levels, even when the deer population is quite low, can be difficult. That is true even if the deer are causing few problems in other farm crops, and the effects are particularly apparent where the soil is not very fertile, and the fields are near suitable cover. The deer which are in the area will visit the maize and exploit the resource determinedly, and their constant presence can cause substantial damage. So, what advice should deer managers offer to farmers and estate owners where maize growing is planned?

First you need to consider the overall state of the deer population. The deer manager will have his own opinion on that, as will the farmer, and if the deer manager has been operating to defined objectives both parties will have opinions as to whether these objectives have been, or are being, achieved, quite apart from the maize situation. Good record keeping and annual reports will have helped give the owner confidence in what the deer manager is doing, and an established and stable relationship is the key to surviving a 'maize crisis'.

A second, and vitally important factor is the location where the maize is planted. If deer management is embedded in the overall estate management, as in my view it should be, then it is wise for the farmer or farm manager to consult the deer manager each year when the crop planting is being planned. Good advice at this stage could anticipate any problems, and effective advance planning should minimise damage. I can illustrate how this can work with two examples of what happened on the same estate in Dorset.

In the first instance the deer manager was told that a certain field was to be planted with maize. This was some years ago, and it was my first experience with that particular crop. The stalking team set up highseats and watched the field at regular intervals. The first thing that happened was that a flock of rooks spent some days attacking the newly sown seed. Then the resident rabbit population started on the edges of the field as the crop germinated. Finally the deer moved in; and throughout that summer the field had a resident group of both roe and sika. Although the damage they caused was of little economic significance, we shot several deer, concentrating the summer cull for that part of the estate in this single, but very large, field, more to give the farming tenant confidence that we were doing something than anything else.

It is worth noting that although the field was relatively large in relation to others in this area, it was fairly exposed, and was wooded only along its longest and highest edge. The adjacent woodland was on a steep and narrow slope above the field, and was rather open and not very attractive to deer. Consequently only the resident roe and sika tended to use this field, and regular shooting had some deterrent effect. The end result was acceptable damage.

Five years later another tenant on the same estate planted a maize field in a totally different situation. He made no attempt to involve the deer manager either by asking his advice at the planning stage or by telling him what had been decided. Thankfully the deer manager noticed what was going on as the crop germinated, and a team of stalkers, including myself, monitored the situation. It was as well that we did.

The site selected was a smallish field of some 13 acres (5.25 hectares). Surrounded on two and a half sides by woodland, it provided security and ready access to dense cover. The woodland is mature, with Scots pine about seventy years old mixed with a scattering of oak, birch and sweet chestnut. The soil is a thin grey podzol; the field had probably been reclaimed from heathland in the dim and distant past. Ever since I can remember it has been a haven for deer, and groups of twenty to thirty sika are common at certain times of the year. The woodland floor is covered with a dense mat of rhododendron, and so the deer have ample security, shelter and comfortable lying-up within 30 or 40 yards of the field edge. It would be difficult to select a field where the potential for deer damage on maize would be greater. Although the stalking team was satisfied that the population of both sika and roe was acceptable, and that there had been no substantiated complaints about deer damage on agricultural crops for some time, it was clear that this was about to change. Furthermore, a nearby area of heathland had recently been sheep fenced to encourage grazing for conservation, and it was becoming clear that this had also altered the habits of the local deer quite substantially. The scene was set for problems.

It rapidly became obvious that a strip about 15 metres wide at the southern edge of the field was suffering from poor germination, whether from bad planting or being perpetually in shade we could not tell. The crop simply never thrived there. That was bad enough, but then there were badgers. One of my colleagues counted seventeen on one evening, and they were pulling the maize stems down to get at the ripening cobs. All of this happened before we even began to experience deer damage. Very few roe used the field but the same could not be said of the sika. The average number feeding on any one visit was seventeen, both stags and hinds, and

Above: Pressure for public access continues to increase, New Forest, 1995. (RM)

Below: 200 hectares were vulnerable to deer at any one time (see page 42). (RM)

Above: An adult roe deer in summer coat, Wareham Forest, July 1996. (RM)

Below: Roe buck changing into summer coat, Dorset, May 1996. (RM)

Above: Roe doe in full summer coat, Dorset, 1993. (RM)

Below: Sika hinds and calves, Isle of Purbeck, Dorset. (RM)

Above: A young roe doe emerging cautiously from cover, Dorset, June 1996. (RM)

Below: A roe kid concealed amongst brushwood on the forest floor. (RM)

Left: Stubble turnips eaten by roe in winter. (RM)

Below: Sika stag in velvet, Isle of Purbeck, Dorset, July 1996. (RM)

Above and below: Fallow bucks can be aged from their antlers (RM)

Above: Red stags follow their chosen hinds during the rut, New Forest, 1995. (RM)

Below: Fallow buck during the rut, New Forest, 1997. (RM)

Above: The typical group is a hind, yearling and calf. Sika photographed in Wareham Forest, Dorset. (RM)

Maize, growing well. (SV)

Maize suffering from shade or poor planting. (RM)

Maize plants doing well. (SV)

Maize plant eaten by sika. (RM)

the numbers recorded varied from six to thirty. They fed repeatedly, taking the fresh centres out of many stems. By the time the crop was harvested the total yield may have been down by as much as 40 per cent, of which the stalkers estimated perhaps half had been caused directly by deer, the other half being a combination of badger damage and poor take.

As soon as the stag open season started the stalkers took several of the poorer individuals from the field – in fact 80 per cent of the stag cull for that year was taken in three weeks during August – something that we have never done before, and hope never to do again. By that time however, the damage had been done, and I have no doubt that if the deer population on this estate were to be nearly exterminated, the few survivors would find and exploit a maize crop in that field or others like it.

This demonstrated to me that perhaps the single most important factor in planting maize is to select the location very carefully. Try to select a field with limited access to heavy cover, where there is a chance of making the deer feel insecure. Deer damage to maize cannot, in my view, be contained simply by shooting, in the way that most woodland damage can be. The crop is so attractive that deer will find it, and if there is suitable cover nearby they will be virtually impossible to dislodge. Other repellent techniques such as the use of bangers (bird scarers) are other similar devices can be helpful in making the deer feel unwelcome, but in most cases the effects last for only a short time until the deer get used to them. I have heard recently that some farmers, in an attempt to minimise loss by deer in maize crops, are resorting to sowing widths of 10 feet (3 metres) around their field margins with low-grade maize seed. The thinking behind this approach is to reduce costs and contain financial loss within the most vulnerable areas, whilst still providing some harvestable material. I would think that more would be gained from better selection of the chosen sites coupled, wherever the farmer has the right to control deer, with careful and targeted deer management.

By far the most important aspect of dealing with damage to any kind of crop is the ability of the deer manager to attribute that damage correctly, in other words to lay the blame at the proper source. It is not easy, and invariably involves judgement and knowledge in about equal measure. It is a subject with which I still struggle, and requires a 'nature detective' approach – building up to a conclusion from the often scanty information. It is obviously unhelpful for deer to be blamed for damage caused by other factors. As we have seen, browsing and grazing damage can be caused by rabbits, hares or sheep. And even if the deer are responsible, a decision still has to be made as to whether the damage is likely to have been caused by the population being too high, or by another factor such as unusually severe and long-lasting weather or the crop being in a deer hot spot.

It can sometimes be useful to look at the motivation of the various parties involved. I recall a case where a lot of young trees went brown and died quite suddenly. It was difficult to be sure of the cause, and the word 'deer' was being bandied about rather consistently by the forest staff. Thankfully, the stalker involved had a good reputation and, more importantly, had kept good records, not only of his own work but also of the area as he had watched it being planted. A few well-placed enquiries confirmed that the trees had been left exposed to the weather for several days on site, and that the standard of planting was also very poor. Obviously this was embarrassing for the resident forester, and it was extremely tempting for him to suggest that deer were the cause. At the very least this would confuse the issue and dissipate the blame, but it might also shift the responsibility totally. Because the stalker had noted in his diary the various factors which he had observed, responsibility was finally attributed where it really belonged, but less diligence might well have resulted in a very different conclusion. More young trees probably die as a result of poor handling and inadequate storage than from direct deer damage, but the effects are often not easily discernible, since they do not usually become obvious for several weeks after planting, when the trees finally die.

There are deer hot spots where damage will occur, regardless of the level of the population, and once these areas are identified, suitable protection should be provided if tree planting is considered essential. It is difficult to be sure what makes a certain site a hot spot, but probably the availability of nearby, secluded daytime cover is a key factor. It is difficult to decide when the problem is caused by too high a population or by a hot spot, but if you know from past culling levels that your population is quite low, and if the damage is isolated and recurs regularly in the same area, the problem is likely to be a hot spot. Otherwise I would assume a population problem, and step up the cull accordingly.

In the final analysis it is important that damage caused by deer or as a result of deer is attributed to them, and no responsible deer manager should seek to evade responsibility for that; but it is equally important, if deer management is to be improved, that damage caused by other factors is attributed to them and not to deer.

4.
AUTUMN FOR THE WOODLAND DEER MANAGER

Roe in autumn

As the long days of summer begin to draw to a close and the nights get noticeably cooler and we begin to think of lighting the fire, so the habits of the deer change. For herd deer the autumn rut is the time of renewal, of mating, when primeval forces take over and the urge to reproduce becomes irresistible. For roe bucks the autumn simply means antler casting, perhaps with a little delayed mating action through what is normally known as the false rut, whilst for females of all species it means a time to fatten up as far as possible, in order to be able to sustain both their dependent young and the developing embryos within them throughout the coming winter.

There seems little doubt that although most roe does are covered by the buck during the normal rut in late summer, a few, presumably those which were not covered properly or at all, do come into oestrus again later, and most of these are covered at that time. However, most roe bucks will start to cast their antlers as November comes in, and although some will still carry one or perhaps both antlers well on into December, most will have cast long before then. It would be logical to assume that once a buck has cast, with his testosterone level at its lowest, he will no longer be capable of inseminating an available female, so presumably females which are unmated by early December remain barren for that year. However, the term 'false rut' is a misnomer; it assumes something unusual or out of the ordinary, whereas mating outside the peak period is simply the covering of a receptive female which may have come into season at a different time. It happens with most deer species, and it explains the unusual occurrence of very young deer at times when, in theory, there should not be any.

So autumn is a quiet time in the roe calendar, and most serious stalkers will have completed their buck cull before or during September, and will be unable to start the female cull until the open season begins on 1 November. However, muntjac stalkers will still be busy; their season never ends. And stalkers who deal with the herd deer (fallow, sika and red) will be approaching one of the most interesting and instructive times of their year – the rut of these species.

Herd deer in autumn

During the last half of August, male red, sika and fallow deer will have been busy cleaning their new antlers and getting into prime breeding condition. This process

Red deer in the New Forest. (VP)

Sika Stag during the rut, October 1995. Isle of Purbeck, Dorset. (RM)

can start at the beginning of the month, but by the end of August most stags and bucks will be clean. The hardening of antlers and consequent cleaning is controlled by the rise of testosterone to its peak, and following cleaning the male is in prime breeding condition. Since male herd deer grow their antlers during the summer, in a time of plenty, there is a much closer correlation between antler growth and the quality of the male in question than there is with roe, which grow their antlers during winter, where shelter, food and climate can have a considerable effect.

Among the herd deer therefore, any male which exhibits poor-quality antlers should be a candidate for culling, provided that this fits in with the rest of the plan. There is need for caution here, because it is not easy to judge age in the field. I remember shooting a sika stag many years ago, which I selected out of a bunch of about fifteen because it appeared to me to be a poor four-pointer, with six- and eight-pointers around it. I judged this to be its second head. Eric Masters, looking at it later, said that in his opinion it was a pricket (first head) and therefore of exceptional quality. You live and learn. Sika stags are very difficult to age by their antlers. Many commonly carry six points at the second head stage, whilst others have six throughout their lives. Yet others develop eight points by, say, the third head, and then grow steadily larger until the age of, say, ten, after which they tend to 'go back'. There seems to be no close correlation between number of points and age.

Red deer are very similar, albeit with much larger antlers, which carry many more points. There are great differences between hill reds (which live in bleak and inhospitable places like the Scottish Highlands) and lowland reds such as those living in the forests and farmlands of East Anglia, the New Forest or in the West Country, in respect both of body weight and size and antler development and growth. Whilst it is often possible to identify an individual stag by his antlers, usually assisted by the location in which he is observed, so far as I am aware it is not possible to age one accurately by reference to his antlers. As I said in Chapter 3, the only reliable way I know of ageing wild deer successfully is through tooth sectioning or where deer of known age have been clearly marked. The first method requires a dead animal and a rather time-consuming process, and the second is normally only possible when deer either begin their lives in captivity or are caught as juveniles and collared or ear-tagged. Even then the tags need to be identifiable from a distance under field conditions.

Fallow are rather easier to age in the field, since antler development follows pre-ordained stages. The complication for the field observer or stalker is then being able to distinguish between good and poor development within each age class. Males are given different names at each stage, and these names are:

- pricket – first head fully developed at fifteen months and carried to twenty-three months
- sorel – second head fully developed at twenty-seven months and carried to thirty-four or thirty-five months
- sore – third head fully developed at thirty-nine months and carried to forty-six or forty-seven months
- bare buck – fourth head fully developed at fifty-one months and carried to fifty-eight or fifty-nine months

A menil fallow buck (in captivity). (RM)

- buck – fifth head fully developed at sixty-three months and carried to seventy or seventy-one months
- great buck – sixth and subsequent heads.

From this development process, coupled with the demeanour of the animal, it is usually possible to place fallow bucks within the correct age classification – certainly until the buck and great buck stages are reached, at which time relative classification may be more difficult.

Selection of males for culling

As far as practical field guidelines are concerned I have found that a good approach to selecting for the cull, regardless of species, is to start with the stalker's best assessment of each male encountered, followed by his best assessment of whether it should be classified as good, poor or reasonable. This assessment will have to be based on a judgement of its age and its condition relative to that age. Factors to be taken into account will include the animal's body size and condition, its demeanour and its antler growth. Unusual local factors may also need to be considered, if local

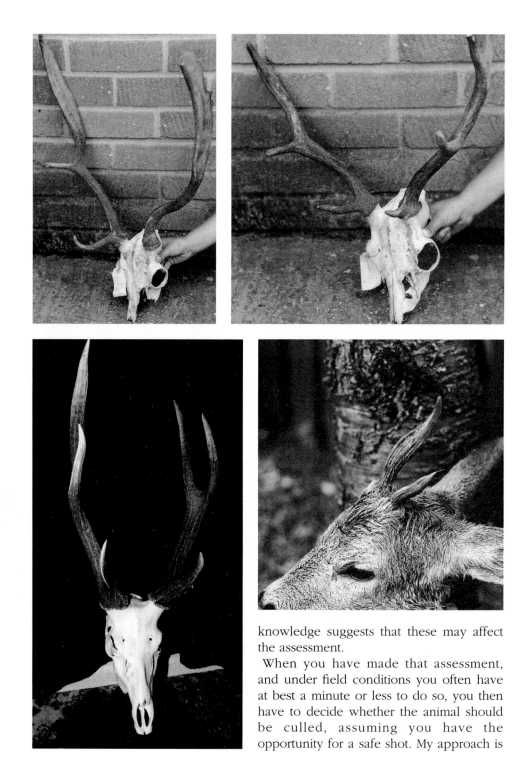

Poor antlers – fallow, cull. (RM)

Far left: Poor antlers – sika, cull. (RM)

Poor antlers – roe, cull. (RM)

knowledge suggests that these may affect the assessment.

When you have made that assessment, and under field conditions you often have at best a minute or less to do so, you then have to decide whether the animal should be culled, assuming you have the opportunity for a safe shot. My approach is that I will always shoot an animal which I consider to be poor, regardless of the progress of my cull plan. An animal which I classify as good, I will always leave. And for reasonable animals, I decide whether to shoot according to how my plan is progressing. Sometimes you will be dealing with a population which contains a high proportion of good-quality males, and few poorer animals. In that case I would shoot the poorest of the males I came across (notwithstanding that these might be classed as good in many populations), up to my cull plan.

At the end of the day a great deal comes down to personal judgement. You will make mistakes, but the important thing is to learn by them. At least you will be trying to make progress, and in doing so will further your own deer management objectives. Above all, be honest with yourself. It is easy to make misleading or untrue reports because generally you are alone, without witnesses. I maintain that if I chose to do so, I could fool many people regarding deer, much of the time. However, what is the point of that except to bolster my ego? If we are really trying to improve deer management we should strive towards truth. That means recognising our mistakes and trying not to repeat them.

The autumn rut for herd deer

The autumn rut is my favourite time of the year as far as deer are concerned, although I shoot very few at this time. I love the cold dawns, often followed by sunshine and clear skies, with the russets, reds and browns of the autumn woods. It is also the time when the deer are at their most vocal – fallow grunting (belching), sika whistling, red bellowing. What more can any stalker want?

The first sika stag in this part of Dorset is usually heard before September is many days old, the clear triple whistle carrying far in the crisp, early autumn air. Occasionally one starts whistling in August, but for much of September the pattern

There is a hierarchical order when sika stags take and hold territories. (RM)

is of an occasional call from an individual stag. As October begins the intensity and frequency of the calls increase, and it is common to hear several stags whistling one after the other. Sika are amazingly vocal, and a wide range of calls have been recorded and described by different observers. For the purpose of this book I will restrict myself to the two most common: the triple (or quadruple) whistle and the moaning call.

The best-known call of the sika stag is the triple whistle – a piercing, far-carrying and unearthly sound which many observers cannot believe comes from a deer. It is possible to imitate the call, and one way of doing so was pioneered by Eric Masters, who used the 'squeakers' from his children's toys, blowing into them through cupped hands, and regulating the sound by the strength of his blow, and the width at which he held his fingers. The moaning call is nearly as common. It sounds rather like the bleating of a sheep in distress, but it is much deeper and more penetrating than that of any sheep. There is a distinct bleating quality to it, however, and it ends with a short rasping tone as though the stag has suddenly run out of breath. As far as I know, nobody has perfected an imitation of this call.

Stags use both calls more or less at random – at least I have never been able to discern any pattern. The triple whistle carries for a long distance – often up to a mile – whilst the moan, being lower and quieter, carries less. Both calls are uttered with little or no warning, and like the alarm shriek of female sika are particularly penetrating. If blasted from dense cover both have an eerie effect, and I confess that the hairs on the back of my neck stand upright when I am nearby.

Sika stags take and hold territories, and there is a hierarchical order during this process. Nobody really knows what makes the ideal territory but my guess is that its value is related to its position in relation to the daily movement of the hinds across their home range, with secondary factors such as seclusion and the availability of suitable lying-up cover also playing a part.

Stags eat and drink relatively little during the peak of the rut, which may last for three weeks, and it is therefore no wonder that they lose condition rapidly. A spent sika stag at the end of the rut can easily weigh twenty or thirty pounds (9–14 kg) less at the end of the rut than he did at the beginning. The rut is a time of constant activity for male deer, taking and holding their territory, discouraging rivals (sometimes by force), and serving the hinds as they become available and receptive. Fights between rival males are fairly common, though one does not often witness one. Injuries are quite common and although fatalities have been recorded I have never seen one. I have a record of a sika stag which Eric secured for a client some years ago, which had lost an eye and which also had a broken antler tine embedded in its head, near the pedicle.

Within a man-made forest sika stags tend to use forest roads, tracks and rides as boundaries for their territories, and during the rut they can sometimes be seen thrashing at heather or similar rank vegetation, perhaps out of frustration. It is a comical sight to see a stag with a mass of vegetation hanging from his antlers. It is quite usual to have several stags all whistling one after the other in adjacent territories, but although a resident male will simply not tolerate older stags, younger ones are frequently ignored. This is presumably because they do not present a

Red stags follow their chosen group of hinds during the rut. (RM)

significant challenge to the resident stag's supremacy, probably because they may be too immature to breed successfully.

Whilst there are similarities in the rutting process of the different species of herd deer, there are also sharp contrasts. Red stags follow their chosen groups of hinds as they go about their daily routine, mating whenever the opportunity arises, whilst fallow bucks hold a territory and rarely leave it as long as they are undisturbed by humans. Within that territory, known as a rutting stand, the stand buck holds his group of does for as long as he can, chivvying them constantly and patrolling to prevent rivals from getting near them. The does can be held within the stand for long periods, sometimes days at a time, and mated as they come into season. Sika share some characteristics of both red and fallow. Stags hold a territory but the daily routine of the hinds remains unaltered during the rut. It is my belief, from our observations, that the stags which get most mating opportunities are probably those which hold territories in areas where the hinds spend quite a lot of time, probably near their feeding or lying-up locations. There seems little doubt that sika hinds travel through various territories as they move to their night time feeding areas and back again at dawn, and are presumably covered when receptive by the resident stag which happens to be in that territory at that time.

Whistling goes on throughout October, even well into December, although by this time the frequency is much reduced and only the occasional stag is heard. The period of actual mating extends well outside the peak period of the rut, as is evident in the spread of ages of young animals seen from time to time. The vast majority are born during late May and early June, but the variation can be quite wide. Eric Masters shot a hind and calf on 29 November 1983 in Wareham Forest, Dorset, with the calf still in its baby coat, and therefore no older than ten to twelve weeks, which would put the birth date between 1 and 20 September. Assuming a normal pregnancy, mating would have taken place late in January or early in

February. This is the most extreme example I have come across, but it demonstrates the wide, if occasional, variations which are often found when dealing with deer.

Fallow bucks become vocal a little later than sika. In Devon, 10 October was often taken as the usual date when groaning would begin, but it probably varies in different years and in different regions. I do not think the period when fallow bucks are most vocal varies as widely as the calling period of sika, and in some years the fallow rut is fairly quiet, while in others prolonged and regular groaning occurs for up to three weeks. I believe that the fallow rut peaks in most years around 18–23 October, when activity is at its height. I will always remember one morning, many years ago, in the upper Teign valley in Devon, when I stood at a vantage point at first light and listened to the forest awakening below me. As the mist slowly rolled back, exposing first the tall conifers which clothed many of the steep slopes and then the shorter, stunted old oaks which were relics of the native vegetation in the valley, I heard the first buck belch in the valley below. As I tuned in to the forest sounds another buck replied from a steep goyle a little to the west, and before I could work out exactly where he was, another sounded off far below. Finally I located seven different animals all groaning vigorously, and later in the morning, I found every buck on his rutting stand, and identified each one. Although I carried my trusty .270, I never fired a shot, nor was I detected by any deer during that whole process, and it remains one of the highlights of a lifetime's work with deer.

On a different occasion in the same valley, in Alan's early days with me, we got within fifteen feet (5 metres) of a stand buck – so close that we could clearly see his enlarged eye glands even in the poor light under the spruce plantation. As he

Calling a sika stag using the 'squeaker' from a child's toy. (JJM)

belched we could almost feel the blast of air which was being expelled and the vibration had to be sensed to be believed. That, I believe, is the closest that I have ever been to a rutting buck although Eric recalls an instance when he shot a sika stag which he had called for a client, when it was eight yards away and coming quite aggressively. The client was still busy looking at the stag through his binoculars. As Eric said afterwards, 'I didn't think he would be able to react quickly enough, and I could see one of us getting speared.' I think it was the only time in his long career that Eric took such dramatic action, and it does demonstrate that the autumn rut is a time to take care, for male deer lose much of their natural fear of humans when the mating urge is rampant.

I had a similar experience the very first time I called a stag for a client. The gentleman concerned was a German hunter, and I had quietly approached a likely spot and called. Before I got the whistle back in my pocket – in fact I was still holding it – the stag appeared. He was coming up the plough furrows on which the pine crop had been planted like a pointer, with head forward. I nudged the client and nodded in the stag's direction, checking quickly with my binoculars to ensure that it was shootable, although I was pretty sure from the location and a brief glimpse that it was the territorial stag, and the beast that we were after. When I looked at the client again the stag was less than twenty yards away and looking at us. The client was fully occupied studying the animal through his binoculars, with his rifle still slung on his shoulder. When I caught his eye I tried to indicate that he should shoot, without making any more movement than was absolutely necessary. The stag trotted off, perhaps another fifteen yards, and was now presenting a classic broadside shot at about thirty yards. 'Surely' I thought, 'nothing can go wrong now, and this will be a great "first" for me.' How wrong I was. The hunter was still looking at the stag through his binoculars, his rifle still slung on his shoulder. Finally the stag got fed up and ambled off through the forest. Afterwards I was trying to explain that in our man-made forests it is often necessary to shoot fairly quickly if you are to secure a shot, and I asked why he didn't even get his rifle ready. 'I was assessing the quality of the beast,' he replied. Much closer, I thought, and he might have been assessing our quality, but with customer/client relationship in mind I kept those thoughts to myself.

Before rushing out to try your hand at calling during the rut, heed a few words of caution. Bill Hendy had a nasty experience many years ago on the Haldon Hills just outside Exeter, in Devon. He was checking rutting fallow bucks as dusk began to fall, and was creeping quietly through a gorse thicket which formed an open space within the forest at this point. A fallow buck groaned in the forest to one side. Bill thought that he would have a bit of fun and groaned back. A second buck started behind him, and then a third from the next plantation. Before Bill knew what was happening he could hear antlers thrashing the gorse within a few yards, and he was caught between the three bucks. It was nearly dark and visibility, already limited amongst the gorse, was down to perhaps 5 yards. It was the only time in his long career with deer that Bill ever confessed to feeling really afraid. 'I really thought that I was going to have to shoot one or two of them in order to get out of there, and I had my rifle ready,' he said afterwards, but as it happened they

Before rushing out to try your hand at calling, heed a few words of caution. A massive fallow buck during the rut can appear quite intimidating. (RM)

eventually settled down and with some relief Bill finally got back to the safety of the open forest road.

When approaching deer during the rut it is not the males that you need to be most careful about – they are usually somewhat preoccupied. It is the females, who rarely if ever relax; and when one does, another assumes responsibility for watching. I have a set of antlers on my wall, and the story of how those were taken illustrates the point. It was in Devon during the autumn rut in 1984. It was one of the first times that I had taken Teal, my labrador (who was to become so important to our team and our set-up), out stalking with me. He had proved steady to heel

Teal – the labrador who was to become so much a part of our team – finding a deer for Alan Lewis. (RM)

Ears turning through 360 degrees – in this case a sika hind (RM)

and shown an interest, and he had found two or three shot deer. I decided that it would be a good idea to take him with me instead of having to walk back 2 or 3 miles in order to fetch him if he was needed. The fallow rut was in full swing and as we descended along a steep track I heard a brief grunt on the opposite slope. Softly, one step at a time, we crept along until we reached a point where the valley opened out slightly in front of us. I watched but all was still and quiet, and I was on the point of deciding to move on – a decision which would have wrecked the stalk – when Teal suddenly inhaled sharply. Later I recognised that as being his way of telling me that he had scented a deer, but at this stage in our relationship I was mystified because I could see nothing. I stayed very still and watched. Finally, after several minutes of total inaction my patience was rewarded with a tiny movement amongst the huge rocks which littered the area. The glasses revealed a fallow doe, ears turning through an arc of nearly 360 degrees as she tried to locate the noise which had alerted her – presumably the slight noise when I had taken a single step forward. As I watched, others revealed themselves until I could count eighteen does and prickets. As they relaxed and began to move around again I watched in fascination as the scene started to unfold before me.

The acrid belch of the master buck confirmed where he was. He had been about a hundred yards away, and had returned to this group of does ready to resume his mating quest. Still Teal and I watched, and finally he revealed himself and I was able to confirm that he was shootable. Over a period of eight years or so we had improved the quality of antlers in this fallow herd quite considerably. The heads had been very poor, although body weights were good. By following a strict policy of shooting as many substandard males as possible within our overall cull targets, and by not shooting any males we considered to be above average, we had created a situation where there were reasonable numbers of good males of all ages in the herd; and where, more importantly, there were very few poor ones. It was my first real experience of what could be achieved by selective culling. In this, our ninth year, we had decided that we could afford to take one reasonable buck each, to have one good set of antlers each as a permanent reminder of what we had achieved. In order to keep the number of bucks in reasonable balance some good bucks would have to be taken anyway, since the poor ones had been rigorously removed in past years.

The buck which I had found was a year or so short of his prime, and although a nice head was nothing exceptional. I decided therefore that he could be shot. The next question was how to achieve this. In the event it proved quite easy – a standing shot, using my stick, at about 130 yards. The stricken buck ran uphill away from me, but conveniently fell on the top woodland ride. Even retrieving the carcase would be straightforward, and my morning's work was virtually done. However, were it not for Teal I would never have got in a position to get that shot at all. He had located the 'ladies on watch', and in doing so had provided me with another lesson which I have never forgotten – you can sometimes take liberties and get away with them with male deer, but you will rarely do so with females. The maternal instinct is extremely strong, and the stalker would be well advised not to forget it.

Fallow bucks will fight during the rut, and over the years I have watched quite a few encounters. Three remain clear in my mind. The first was during October 1966, and took place in the Forest of Dean in Gloucestershire. This was long before I started stalking, although I was studying a herd of fallow in my spare time even then. I quote from my diary:

'Two fallow bucks emerged from cover to a clear patch of ground not far from us. They stood motionless and surveyed the air currents with nostrils twitching. With a deft movement one buck prodded the other with his antlers and the fight began. The second whirled and, antlers locking with a fearful clash, the beasts began pushing and wheeling furiously. Through our field glasses we could see the immensely powerful leg and neck muscles rippling and straining in the first strong rays of the morning sun. They were fine animals, evenly matched in size and build, with similar heads, one buck having a cleft in the left palm.

'They fought and fought, pausing only to sniff the air and ascertain that there was no outside interference. Then their heads would lower again, as if by mutual agreement, and the little glade would resound once more to the clash of antler upon antler.

'For what seemed an eternity we watched enthralled as neither male would concede victory to his opponent. Then as suddenly as the fight had begun, it ended, as "cleft antler" turned and fled. On checking our watches we saw that twenty-six minutes had elapsed since the opening of this drama.

'The victor strode up and down the clearing uttering his weird rutting call, whilst we returned happily to our breakfast content at having been privileged to witness this incredible scene. It is perhaps easy to see why I have been enthralled by deer for so much of my life.'

Later, in Devon, I was to see several more fights among fallow bucks, and also gain an appreciation of the damage which they could do. With a close friend I watched a fight during the 1979 rut, which also lasted in excess of twenty minutes, and again it was easy to feel the sheer aura of strength of the combatants. On examining the forest floor afterwards we found the leaves were churned up as though they had been ploughed. On that day we had been alerted to what was happening by hearing the first clash of antlers, and had gradually worked our way nearer, until we had a 'ringside seat' at a distance of perhaps 60 yards.

In 1978 I had another glimpse of the results of the struggle for supremacy among fallow. I had been instructed to shoot a nice buck so that the antlers could be mounted for one of the owners of the land. I had protested that we could not spare a nice buck, because at that stage we were rooting out all the substandard males, and had very few nice bucks to breed. The forester was insistent, so I decided to leave it as late in the rut as possible, on the basis that if I had to shoot a nice buck he might at least have chance to pass on his genes to the next generation, and also to prevent a poorer animal being able to capitalise on his removal. I picked an area where I knew that a nice buck was rutting, but after searching for over two hours I found nothing. Finally I spotted a deer in the oakwood on the slope above me, which proved to be a big buck that I recognised from the previous year, when he had been on a rutting stand nearby. He had no does in attendance, and I knew that the traditional rutting stand in the area was on the lower slopes a few hundred yards below, so something strange was obviously going on.

The shot was uneventful, but later, while skinning the beast, I discovered why he was not on the stand. Along his backbone on the left side were five holes, into which I could fit my finger to a depth of perhaps 2 inches (5 centimetres). Obviously this buck had been injured, but it was not until the following year, when I witnessed the fight just described that I found out how the injury had been caused. As the beaten buck in that encounter had turned away the victorious animal had stabbed viciously at its hindquarters with his massive antlers. The brow tines had been used like short spears, stabbing the fleeing buck without mercy, and the force of the attack was quite sufficient to penetrate the thick skin of the loser, and cause these deep wounds. In this case my bullet had killed it before infection set in, but it is easy to understand what could happen as a result of such a determined attack.

I wondered what buck had displaced this fine animal from his stand status, so at dawn the next morning I was back in this wood, on the edge of the rutting stand. The new stand buck was enormous, black in colour with a superb head, and was clearly wasting no time in asserting his supremacy. Over the following eight seasons

I got to know him well. I located him in seven ruts, and could have shot him on many occasions, but always chose not to. Recently I listened to an interesting lecture by Steve Smith who has carried out very detailed studies of fallow deer in the New Forest. He has recorded that when fallow bucks assume master buck status, they rarely stay in command of a rutting stand for more than two seasons, by which time they are replaced by a younger and more vigorous animal. I have not studied them in the same detail as Steve, but my experience in the wilder woods of Dartmoor is rather different, as the above story shows. I am sure that this was the same animal, and I am also sure that he successfully returned to this same rutting stand for at least seven years, and was still in fine condition at the end of this period. Quite possibly the competition was less intense because we had been steadily reducing the overall population to fairly low levels when compared with the relatively high density of fallow which are to be found in the New Forest. Whatever the reason, it demonstrates once again the constant and amazing variety to be found when working with wild deer.

The rut of red deer varies in some respects from that of both fallow and sika. Red stags tend to follow chosen groups of hinds wherever they go during the rut, trying to hold the hinds in order to mate. The stag could reasonably be described as less tied to a location or territory, but the essential principle of being the dominant male which gets the best mating opportunities is exactly the same.

When the rut is over – or at least when the main rutting activity finishes – the woods go quiet. It is as though the deer are worn out, and they probably are. Where they go no one is really sure, but before long groups of males are to be seen feeding together, all aggravation over until the following year. Mature males of herd deer seem to live together quite happily outside the rutting period, and there seems to be little animosity between them. The females now develop an urge to find plenty of food, to store fat for the coming winter, and usually at this time of the year the woods are full of fallen fruit, berries, acorns, mast and fungi, all of which attract the deer. It is a time of plenty, with leaner times to come soon. For the stalker there is a brief respite before the really important work of deer control begins in earnest – the female cull.

The season for the female cull begins on 1 November (except for muntjac which have no legally binding close season). For very good reasons I advocate that most stalkers should start this task as early as possible, and whilst I know that November is technically still autumn, I nevertheless regard this as the start of the winter programme.

5.
WINTER FOR THE WOODLAND DEER MANAGER

With the trees losing their leaves and the days getting shorter there is no doubt that winter is on the way. Food, which has been so plentiful for the deer, now becomes harder to find, and they have to forage longer to get the nutrition they need. Even when they find food in quantity the nutritional value is low and the winter spiral of having to expend more energy in order to keep warm whilst existing on poorer food of lower nutritional value has begun. In a hard winter anything which represents food may be eaten, but in normal southern winters when deer numbers are reasonably low, little damage should be done. Holly forms an important constituent of winter food, and often gives a useful indicator of browsing pressure.

The task facing the stalker changes in November, when the open season for female deer begins – except with muntjac and Chinese water deer which have no legal close seasons. Chinese water deer will only affect a tiny proportion of stalkers because of their limited distribution, and overall muntjac control has already been discussed in Chapter 3, so the rest of this chapter is devoted to roe, sika, fallow and red winter management.

I hope that I have made a strong case for planned and targeted deer management, and as I have said there is little doubt that the only way in which deer

Holly forms an important part of the winter food intake for many deer. (RM)

populations can be manipulated effectively is through regulating the female population. The winter period therefore represents the key period in the deer manager's year. It is, furthermore, the time when daylight hours are short, the weather is often unpredictable or inclement, carcase retrieval becomes most difficult because of difficult ground conditions, and everything conspires against the deer manager. Bill Hendy used to say that the female cull sorted out the men from the boys, although in those days when I was young and very keen I did not really appreciate the significance of that remark. It is not just going out on a cold, wet winter's day that is the challenge, it is doing it day after day,

Carcase retrieval can become difficult because of ground conditions. (RM)

. . . or bad weather. (RM)

week after week, year after year, and consistently achieving large female cull programmes. I have the greatest admiration for those dedicated stalkers who can do so, and I say to landowners, land agents and foresters that if they find a stalker or deer manager who can consistently achieve the level of female culling necessary to achieve their management objectives, they should stick with him unless he is, for some other reason, totally unacceptable. Such people are a jewel beyond price. As I get older, and have fewer new experiences in stalking, I find that winter mornings get more difficult. Once out and about I rarely fail to enjoy the outing, but it is convincing myself that there is a better alternative to staying in a nice warm bed that is the problem. Because I am not a full-time stalker my body clock never becomes used to one system of working – it has to adapt to whatever I happen to be doing at the time. Maybe it is this, or maybe it is that the challenge has faded somewhat. Whatever it is, I admire and value the true professionals who can keep on delivering high-quality deer management year after year, for they are dedicated people. Most of them are usually too busy to write about their exploits, but they are the unsung heroes of the deer world, and deer management would be much poorer without them. Those of us who seek to do a good deer management job from the sidelines need to emulate their dedication, although if we are acting as part-timers we do have some choice, and should have much less demanding programmes. I want now to look at what a typical winter deer management programme is all about, and I will start by defining the standard of shooting which is required.

. . . or a long distance from the vehicle. (RM)

Shooting standards for woodland stalking

Many estates and game shoots tend to ban or restrict deer stalking until the game season finishes on 1 February. That leaves the stalker four weeks to achieve the necessary cull. If the cull consists of only three or four does this might be possible, but if the cull is twenty or more then it is very difficult to achieve. It just needs a run of bad weather or a couple of missed shots to really increase the pressure, and that is when things usually start to go wrong.

Shooting is all about confidence. If the stalker has an accurate and reliable rifle, with a good-quality telescopic sight properly zeroed so that the rifle is capable of placing bullets where required, then the ability to hit the target is mainly a mental challenge. In my opinion, many more shots are missed through stalker error than as a result of faulty equipment. This is another instance where a degree of introspection is vital. The ability to be honest with oneself and acknowledge that a mistake has been made is what is needed. I have learned the hard way that any shooting mistake is mine and mine alone, unless I can find a good reason to believe otherwise. Everybody misses or makes a poor shot from time to time – we are all human. But every such occasion should be treated as a learning opportunity and the reason ascertained as far as possible, so that it is not repeated. If you miss most of your shots, or if you consistently fail to get into a proper shooting position, then you should be going back to basics and relearning the necessary skills. If, however, you know that you usually do a decent job, but suffer a string of misses, or a run of poor confidence, then take a rest if possible, and it will come right again in due course.

Shooting is all about confidence. Alan Lewis in his favourite sitting position. (RM)

Use any aids which are available. Eric Masters using a tree as a rest. (RM)

Let me illustrate these points with a couple of examples. During the early 1980s I had a run of consistent successes, regularly pulling off difficult and extremely precise shots. Since I am not naturally a good shot (I have to work very hard at it), I was pleased by this, and began to feel that I was getting somewhere. Then my shooting went to pieces, and it took a long time to get back to that previous peak. I put this down to a particular family problem I had at that time, and it meant that I had to relearn the process, which was very frustrating. I also had to work doubly hard to get myself into an effective shooting position, and then, more often than not, take a body shot, simply because the target area for a killing placement is rather larger than that required for a neck or head shot at the same range. This is one of the secrets of success when stalking deer – learning what you are capable of on the day, in the circumstances in which you find yourself. When you reach that point, you are definitely beginning to improve.

. . and Alan Lewis using a convenient fence. (RM)

Eric Masters once suffered a string of misses – if my memory serves me correctly it was nine in succession. He could never remember missing nine deer in any one season during the whole of his long career, let alone nine in succession. After he had done all of the obvious things like checking his rifle, I told him to take a couple of weeks off stalking. Although this would cause problems in the middle of the winter female cull, I still felt that it was advisable, because such a disastrous sequence has the effect of exaggerating the problem in one's mind. Often a complete rest from the activity is the best way to put it right. In the end Eric only took a couple of days off, but when he shot the next deer he was instantly back to normal. This taught me that it can happen to anyone – previous experience counts for nothing, except that it assists you greatly in putting things right when you have such a problem.

One thing you can do is to use any aids which are at your disposal. A stalking stick or bipod, a standing tree, a stable fence post, a rolled-up roesack or a comfortable sitting position all give greater stability than freehand shooting. I never fire an unsupported shot at a live deer, unless there is a critical need when following up a wounded animal. All other shots are supported in some way, the most common aid being a double stick or bipod. Each stalker has his own preference. Alan, for example, shoots sitting down when he has the chance; this position looks uncomfortable to me, but he likes it and it works for him. Learn not to lose too many shots by moving around to get a better position, unless your quarry is totally unalerted. Learning to balance all of these factors so that you usually make the best decision on the day is part of the challenge of stalking.

The place to ensure that your equipment is properly set up is on a target range, not when aiming at a live animal. After that it comes down to confidence. Alan describes this very well when he says, 'When I am shooting well the rifle snugs into my cheek as though it belongs there, and it seems to line itself up. When I am ready to take the shot the trigger feels like a piece of glass, and it snaps at the instant when I require it to. When things are not going as well, it seems as though I have to pull much harder on the trigger, and I am not sure exactly when it will go off. When I am shooting well I can take neck shots or pick small gaps through foliage with virtual certainty, confident that the shot will be inch perfect. When things are not going as well I have to take more time (possibly missing an opportunity altogether), and I only shoot when I am sure that I have the margin for error I need.' That is good, sound advice. It demonstrates clearly the mental challenge; Alan's trigger pressure will not have changed – it simply feels as though it has.

Over the years I have been privileged to see work by many really excellent rifle shots, Eric Masters was probably the best, with Chris Phillips, Stuart Venables, Jonathan Holmes, Vic Pardy, Mark Warn and Colin Elford close behind. Each of those men is able to assess how they feel on the day and can adjust their shooting accordingly, and they know that they can deliver the goods when it matters, and keep on doing so. Alan and I have shot as many deer as most part-time stalkers, and between us we miss very few, but we are not in the class of these men when it comes to shooting. We therefore have to ensure that our fieldcraft is more than adequate.

A useful attribute for any manager is to be able to assess others by what they do rather than by what they say they will or can do. If evidence is available to back up their claims, then use it. If not, then ask yourself why.

The standard of shooting required for lowland woodland stalking breaks down into two separate but related factors: shot placement and fieldcraft. It is difficult to say which is the most important. I think that I would rate them equally, although there is no doubt that shot placement has a higher profile. It can also be learned much more quickly – developing an adequate standard of fieldcraft takes many years, and maintaining that standard takes a lifetime. Let us look at shot placement first.

Richard Prior set out a shooting standard for woodland stalking which I have not seen bettered in his 1963 book *Roe Stalking* (in the *Shooting Times* Library series). This states:

> The standards needed are not those of a target shooter, and in fact too much target shooting may slow down one's speed because the finger has been trained not to pull the trigger until aim is exact. Few chances will come for a deliberate target-type shot at roe [or other woodland deer]. The whole essence is to get an aimed shot off within reasonable time from any position, standing, kneeling, peering round a tree, or anything but prone and wound into a sling. If under those circumstances you can put your one shot into a four inch target at 100 yards then success is possible providing that you do not get buck fever at the critical moment.

Think about this as you go stalking, and you will realise what a profound statement it is. It covers all aspects of lowland stalking shooting, with the exception of shooting from highseats or from prone positions at long range across open ground.

The place to ensure that your equipment is properly set up is on a target range. (RM)

In both these situations the stalker is usually shooting at a totally unalerted animal, albeit at longer range, and is also shooting from a very steady position. The standard should then be extended to a 4-inch (10-cm) group at 150 yards for those stalkers who graduate to taking these much longer shots.

I once worked out the average range at which I had shot most of my deer, and over a ten-year period this worked out at fractionally over 77 yards (70 metres). The closest shot was at 16 yards (15 metres) and the longest 300 yards (275 metres). Seventy-five per cent of these shots fell within the band between 65 and 130 yards (60 and 120 metres).

Consistent hits on a 4-inch (10-cm) target area will ensure clean kills, provided that the aiming mark is selected accurately. There are plenty of books and training courses which will teach you this, and I do not propose to go into detail here. Suffice it to say that my aiming mark for a body shot at a deer which is standing more or less broadside on is very slightly under halfway up the body and fractionally to the rear of the rear edge of the front leg. That puts the bullet into the mass of internal organs which includes the heart and lungs as well as the major blood vessels which surround them. A shot so placed will ensure a rapid death from shock and loss of blood. Alan and I describe it as the 'boilerworks shot', and mean no disrespect to our quarry in doing so.

When a stalker graduates to neck or head shots, he enters a new phase. There is no doubt in my mind that the body provides the largest target area for a killing shot, and thus the greatest margin for possible error in shot placement. Whilst there is a great deal to be said in favour of neck shots, and a smaller body of opinion in favour of head shots, neither of them is for the novice, and both have severe potential drawbacks which anybody attempting either should understand. They are for highly proficient and experienced practitioners only. When taking a 'boilerworks shot', the bullet which strikes within 2 inches (6 cm) of the aiming mark will still kill the deer cleanly, no matter whether the bullet strikes high, low, front or rear, providing that the aiming mark has been carefully and accurately selected and the target animal is not standing at a very acute angle to the line of shot. Contrast that with, say, a neck shot at a young roe doe, where the killing area at the base of the neck may be no more than 3–4 inches (8–10 cm) wide, and with a high neck shot substantially less. Any error in the placement and execution of the shot is likely to result in a miss. For a head shot – which I do not recommend, although I know several stalkers who use it successfully – the discipline

Consistent hits on a four-inch target area at 100 yards will ensure clean kills. (RM)

required is even higher. The aiming mark is the area of skull which contains the brain. You need to study deer anatomy carefully in order to get a clear picture in your mind before you consider taking such shots – they are most definitely not for anybody who does not have a good knowledge of anatomy. It is essential that the deer is either directly facing the stalker or, even better, looking directly away. Head shots should never be attempted where the head is sideways. It is too easy to smash the jaw, causing a severe but not immediately life-threatening injury from which the animal may escape to die a lingering death much later.

So far we have assumed that the target is, and will remain, perfectly stationary. Whilst that should be the case with the vast majority of deer shot, there will be occasions when the animal will move. If this happens before the point of no return – the instant when your brain transmits the message to your finger to squeeze the trigger – then you can stop. If it happens between the message being sent and the trigger being squeezed, then there is no turning back. With a 'boilerworks shot' there may still be enough margin to provide a fatal shot, though if the deer takes a big step forward the result may be a gut-shot animal which will need a second shot immediately. With a neck or head shot the result may be a miss, but worse it may be a severe but not immediately life-threatening injury. This is every stalker's worst nightmare.

There are no easy answers, no situations which are always right, when dealing with deer. It can be argued that a miss at a neck shot is better than a gut-shot animal which results from a poorly placed body shot or from the deer moving at the moment of firing. The problem is that it is impossible to predict the results in advance. All I can do is to point out to you the ways in which you can use any advantages that are open to you to achieve a satisfactory result, and that means providing yourself with the best possible margin for error. The overriding objective should be to reduce suffering to an absolute minimum. Two stories illustrate how small the margin for error can be.

On one occasion I had selected a sika hind from a group of seven or eight animals which had stopped briefly whilst crossing a forest rackway. She was standing slightly apart from the others, and I lined up a quick 'boilerworks shot'. I saw her move forward as I fired, but I was unable to stop myself. I knew it was a gut shot but she had moved out of sight before I could reload. I waited for about fifteen minutes and moved slowly forward, keeping Teal at heel. He actually winded her, and after several minutes of quiet observation I saw her head behind a dense clump of grass. A carefully placed second shot resolved the matter but she had suffered great distress for fifteen to twenty minutes. To this day I do not think that I could have avoided this, although the memory distresses me, and I find little consolation in the fact that her suffering was almost certainly not due to my error.

On another occasion I finished up with two deer from one shot – again quite accidentally. The second beast (which I had seen and identified but had no intention of shooting), moved forward as I fired. The target animal, a roe doe, stood quite still, but I saw movement as the rifle discharged. Both beasts went down, and it transpired that the bullet had passed through the target animal and killed the other as it passed behind.

The point of these stories is that you should always be honest with yourself. If I know that I have done my best, but have been affected by circumstances beyond my control, then I can live with that. However, if I know that I have fallen below the standard which I set myself, I get upset, and use this as an opportunity to reappraise my attitude, even if the final result has been satisfactory. The standard at which every stalker should be aiming is a cleanly killed deer for every shot fired. You will fall below this standard – that is certain. The test is how often you fall below it, as well as what you do to put things right.

Fieldcraft

Fieldcraft may be taken as the skill necessary to put the stalker in a position where the possibility of a killing shot is high. And in this area, in my opinion, you cannot buy success. You can only achieve it by developing and honing your skills, and this takes time and a great deal of field experience. The basic objective when stalking is to get within 100 yards (preferably 60 or 70) of an unalerted quarry, so that the animal may be identified and related to the cull plan, and a safe shot may be taken if desired. But how do you achieve this? The answer involves a combination of factors, including:

- wearing the correct clothing
- developing the art of quiet movement through woodland terrain
- reading wind direction and currents and responding to changes in them
- knowing the ground and using it to your advantage
- having patience and moving slowly
- developing keen observation and listening skills
- tuning in to your environment
- knowing yourself and responding to your instincts
- combining all of these skills effectively

There may be items in this list which surprise you. I hope so, because one of my objectives is to encourage you to take an enquiring and slightly critical approach.

Everything you wear should be comfortable. Your outer layers should be silent, so that you can walk through a wood without rustling or creaking, or without a loud ripping sound every time you snag a thorn or bramble. This requirement for quiet operation includes your boots. There is a wide range of excellent footwear available and there is really no excuse for any stalker to wear boots which make loud noises. I do not advocate the widespread use of camouflage clothing, particularly where your stalking activities come under any form of public scrutiny. There is no doubt that camouflage clothing, whether the traditional ex-army DPM pattern or the purpose-made camouflaged hunting clothing currently on the market from the USA is effective. However, if you are likely to meet members of the general public, you need to be mindful of the effect which you may have on them – particularly since they may well be people who have little or no appreciation of how the countryside works. If your dress is intimidating or your attitude aggressive, or both, then you could give people completely the wrong impression. They will remember that

Your clothing should be comfortable and silent. (RM)

impression later, when they see country activities portrayed (often inaccurately) in the media, and the countryside will have lost another potential supporter. I therefore strongly recommend not wearing full camouflage clothing, where you are likely to come into regular contact with the general public. I think a camouflage coat with cord or moleskin trousers is entirely acceptable; it is the head-to-toe camouflage attire which I feel gives the wrong impression, especially when coupled with a camouflage veil and a firearm. It gives a strong 'Rambo' impression, and does not predispose people to listen to the compelling arguments about why deer need to be controlled for the good of the countryside. Leave the full camouflage to the professional soldiers and be open with members of the public you meet, especially when they are on public rights of way, and you will be doing your best to bridge the town/country divide. My own preference for lowland stalking clothing includes loden, moleskin or corduroy, but these are personal preferences and there are other good materials around which meet our requirements without making us appear unduly intimidating.

The most important field skill is using the ground. You can walk as silently as you like, but if you are constantly skylined it is a waste of time. Watch how deer use the land to their advantage, and adopt a similar approach. Use small dips and hollows in the ground, and make use of any cover which is available. Keep looking all around you, not only to the front. Never assume that because you have spied an area closely, there is nothing there. Moving a few feet can give an entirely different perspective, and reveal a deer that was previously hidden. Move slowly, watch and listen constantly, and tune yourself in to your surroundings. I reckon it takes me half an hour before I am stalking at my best, and before I lose the traffic noise and hear the small woodland sounds. During that period I need to take even more care.

When you are in tune the terrain tells you things – you can 'feel' the presence of deer. I cannot explain how it happens, I only know that it does and it works. The least sound out of the ordinary alerts you, and often there is simply the feeling that something is about. Do not ignore these feelings; it is your subconscious talking to you. Listen to it. On probably thirty occasions, over the years, my 'inner voice' has told me to change my plan for the stalk and to do something different. My original plan will have taken account of the wind and the prevailing conditions, yet my 'inner voice' will suggest that I fly in the face of common sense. Although this only happens in probably less than 1 per cent of stalks, every time it has happened, and I have followed my instincts, I have found deer.

If you are skylined your stalking is a waste of time. Alan Lewis using the contours very effectively. (RM)

In his early days all Alan saw was white rumps disappearing. (RM)

After about three hours' stalking you may be mentally tired, and that is the time to stop. I try to restrict a single stalk to three hours or less if I can, because I know from experience that when operating at such a peak of concentration that is all that I can manage at the standard which I set for myself.

It is not necessary to walk silently. Every living creature makes some noise. It is adapting the pattern of your noise to the pattern of the woodland which is important. Again, I find this difficult to describe. But sometimes walkers who are oblivious to the presence of deer will be allowed to approach them closely, the deer seem to recognise instantly that there is no threat. Likewise deer are not usually frightened by forest workers with chainsaws or tractors. But they do recognise that a quietly moving individual presents an immediate threat, so by walking and stopping in an irregular pattern, you can often fool them, particularly if, at the same time you use the surroundings to your advantage. This is part of the art of outwitting a wild creature on its own ground, and you can only do it by being receptive and by continually developing your skills.

In his early days of stalking with me, Alan almost gave up. He could not get himself into a shooting position. All he saw was white rumps disappearing into the distance and he felt that he was letting me down. Finally, early in his second season, he started to see deer before they saw him, and from that point on things gradually got better. My experience was different because I had spent many years watching deer before ever shooting one, and so approaching them was not a particular problem for me when I did start shooting. For most people, though, Alan's experience will be typical, so my message is, that if you want to succeed be prepared to serve your apprenticeship and develop your fieldcraft skills.

Alan also had to learn to adapt to working in large-scale woodlands, and his experience in that respect may be of help to others who face the same challenge. I did not even realise that this was a problem for him until he told me several years later. Finding my way around woodlands is second nature to me – in fact I would much rather find my way around an unfamiliar forest than a large town or city. So I gave Alan instructions like 'Go down this ride for about 400 yards (366 metres) until you reach two larch trees. Bear right, downhill through the hemlock, and when you get to the stand of Douglas fir take the middle ride. At the mid-slope level you will find a small patch of red cedar which opens out into a stand of big sitka spruce.' Eventually he told me that he worked it all out by looking for places where the trees changed, and assuming that must be what I had meant. He did not know what the different varieties were, and that had not even occurred to me. Since foresters tend to find their way around woodlands by using such descriptions, they assume that everybody else has similar knowledge. There is also a scale about large forests which can be quite intimidating until you get used to them, and with many aspiring stalkers these days tending to come from a non-rural background, it may be one of the things which presents a big initial challenge. The best advice I can give is always to carry a map of suitable scale, at least until you know the ground and the landmarks. If you get your map from the local forester, ask him to explain what the notations mean. Forestry Commission stockmaps, for example, are difficult to interpret until you learn how to interpret the information provided. Because most man-made forests were originally laid out on some form of grid or rectangular system in order to aid management, however, it is often possible to keep turning in one direction at ride intersections and eventually finish up back where you started. A good sense of direction also helps.

Equipment

You do not need the very latest and most expensive equipment on the market, but it must be of a suitable quality for the task in hand, and you must have the skills necessary to use it to the best advantage. Clothing is a good example. I am amazed how often aspiring stalkers will cheerfully spend large sums on clothing, buying the latest and often most expensive on the market, when more modest items would serve equally well. They are much less prepared to spend the necessary time developing their fieldcraft skills, an investment which would undoubtedly yield much higher dividends in the long run.

There is a whole industry out there which has been geared up to part you from your money, but it is usually better to start with some sound but expendable clothing (such as Army surplus), and then to build up to more expensive items as you identify a need. In that way you will waste very little money and buy only items which will help you to do a good job. You may, of course, choose to buy some expensive clothing simply as a luxury, or perhaps because the cost is not important to you. But do not try to convince yourself that you *must* have this or that item in order to succeed. I have stalked deer to photograph them whilst wearing a fluorescent orange jacket and the stalk was successful. That was simply to prove a point and I would not recommend it, but it helps illustrate that it is your fieldcraft skills which count, not your clothing.

All the rifles which I have used . . . BSA Majestic .270. (RM)

The items which I would never advocate you compromising on are optical aids, be they telescopic sights, camera lenses or binoculars. Always buy the best optics you can afford and skimp elsewhere if you need to. Consider what you want, and for what purpose, and buy accordingly. If you need to economise it is usually better with optics to buy higher-quality but older equipment on the second-hand market, rather than inadequate new gear.

As for rifles, I reckon that all the ones that I have used, from a very cheap .243 many years ago to some very expensive weapons I have fired (though never owned), could shoot better than my capabilities, but a cheap scope which I bought new as a novice lost its zero regularly, and was 'shot out' after six months' use on a .270. I replaced it with a second-hand American scope which nearly broke the bank at the time, but after well over twenty years of heavy use it is still totally reliable today, although rather battered.

Clearly, when buying a used rifle, it is wise to avoid purchasing something which last saw service in the Boer War, or which is 'shot out' or otherwise totally unsuitable for the purpose you have in mind. Believe it or not there are dealers out there who do sell such items. Go to a specialist, and preferably one who stalks himself, and talk over what you want. It is often wise not to buy on your first visit, no matter how tempting the deal offered. Go home and think it over. Buy a suitable calibre for your needs; it is preferable to have a rifle with sufficient knock-down power to do the job under difficult conditions, but there is little point in being over-gunned. If I were buying a new rifle to cope with a range of stalking opportunities, and I wanted one calibre only, I would seriously consider a .308, although there are many other suitable calibres. The .308 is versatile and has relatively low recoil, and a wide range of bullet weights are readily available. What is most important is that the rifle you choose is capable of shooting accurately and has a predictable and smooth trigger action. Try it out before you buy, or at least have it properly demonstrated. It is always important to be clear about your needs before spending a lot of money, otherwise you may end up very disappointed.

The items which you *must* have in order to stalk successfully in the lowlands, as opposed to those which are desirable, are not very many. Assuming that you do not intend to venture out in really poor weather, the essential items are these:

- an accurate and reliable rifle of a legal calibre to shoot deer, which is correctly set up and zeroed for the ammunition which will be used
- a supply of expanding ammunition for that rifle
- a pair of good-quality binoculars
- a sharp knife, preferably with a 'stop' incorporated in the handle
- a length of strong cord or light rope
- comfortable, quiet clothing and a pair of good boots
- a stalking stick or other shooting aid
- a notebook and pencil
- a first aid kit, either portable or in your vehicle
- your firearm certificate or a good quality photocopy, and preferably your permission to be stalking on the land
- some effective insect repellant for summer stalking

Use a stalking stick or other preferred shooting aid . . . in this case a bipod. (RM)

- ear protection of a suitable variety

You should also ensure that somebody knows where you are going and when you are likely to return. Other items may be desirable. My list of these would include the following, but you might wish to add others:

- a spare knife
- a lightweight waterproof suit or poncho which can be carried whilst stalking
- a camera to record items for your diary
- a supply of plastic bags and disposable gloves
- a lightweight hoist and a selection of hooks and gambrels
- a washable and leakproof tray for your vehicle
- an accurate set of scales to weigh carcases
- tags and labels, with indelible pens
- spare, dry clothing to be kept in your vehicle
- identification guides to trees, flowers, butterflies etc.

One item on this list is worth discussing more fully. I learned the value of carrying lightweight waterproof clothing in Scotland, where the estate stalker carried a set of Peter Storm lightweights in his cavernous inner pocket. There are alternative makes available, and in later years I managed to acquire an extremely lightweight American ex-army poncho, which is amazing. It folds to a few square inches, and if I am caught out in a shower (or storm) it covers me, my rifle, binoculars, camera and anything else I am carrying. I have never managed to get another, but similar ponchos are readily available, though not all are as lightweight or tough as mine. I carry it, with a set of light waterproof overtrousers, in a shoulder bag which doubles as a camera bag in which I can also carry a flask of tea. The poncho would also double as an emergency survival bag if that became necessary.

Deer control and game shooting

The interface between stalking and game shooting can present problems, but I have no doubt that a competent and sensible stalker going quietly about his business does no harm at all to a game shoot. Alan and I have carried out deer management on an area with a very fine game shoot for many years and there has never been the slightest conflict. We have often stalked during the week of a shoot, and sometimes on a shooting day, and we have never experienced a problem. Having said that it would be unwise to stalk in the main woods on a shooting day; this is asking for trouble, because if anything goes wrong on the shoot you will probably get the blame. On the very occasional instance where we have stalked on a shooting day, we have always restricted our activities to the outside coverts or the periphery of the shoot. However, I remain convinced that the problems are perceived rather than actual, and revolve around the natural caution and insecurity of keepers during the shooting season. Theirs is a fragile and lonely occupation, and problems become immediately apparent to their employers on shooting days. Everything which could possibly have an adverse affect on the shoot is therefore avoided, and that is a good commonsense approach. But I want to make the point that I do not believe a good stalker will cause any significant problems to a game shoot as a result of deer stalking throughout the game shooting season. I would always advocate that he should avoid shooting days and probably a couple of days beforehand, in order to avoid any potential conflict, but in my opinion that is all that is needed in the vast majority of situations. Moreover some useful fox control may often be carried out, which will of be of direct benefit to the keeper.

If I had been forced to operate with limited stalking – or none at all – during the game shooting season, I could never have achieved many of the objectives outlined in this book. In commercially run forests where game shooting and deer management both take place, the forest managers will normally see deer management as the higher priority; but given sensible liaison between woodland manager, gamekeeper and deer manager, major problems prove to be few and far between in practice. I have shot deer within a few metres of game feed rides, and have invariably found that when I return a few minutes later to collect the shot beast, many of the birds are already back feeding on the feed ride. Stalking, by its very nature, is a quiet activity and the occasional shot has virtually no effect on game, especially later in the season, when numbers are lower anyway.

We start our winter programme every year in early November, and I like to have at least half the planned female cull in the deer larder before the end of that month. Not only are venison prices usually much higher then, but every deer in the larder before Christmas takes me closer to achieving my cull by the end of the season. I also find that December is usually a flat month for deer, particularly fallow. They are usually difficult to find and the daylight hours are at their shortest, and they frequently appear again as the new year begins. December is also the time of the biggest shooting days. Most shoots build up from outside days at the start of the season in October, through the first shoots in each wood during November, peaking with the very best days in December, and then round the season off with days of lower bags in January. Concentrating on the female deer cull during November, easing off during December, and accelerating again during January and February therefore fits comfortably with the typical game shooting pattern found on most estates and game shoots.

I am cautious when I hear of estates which leave deer control to their keepers. At first glance this seems a good plan; it keeps the gamekeeper fully occupied throughout the year and provides excellent value for money. In many cases however, it simply will not work, at least when deer management is being targeted to achieve specific woodland management objectives. I know one or two keepers who balance their objectives fairly successfully, but generally they are extremely competent individuals who have a particular interest in deer, and often have excellent back-up help as well, either voluntary or paid. Much more frequently the two simply do not mix, and the reasons are obvious. The key period when the stalker needs to reduce deer numbers by shooting female deer is exactly the time that the game shoot is in full swing, and the keeper is therefore also under maximum pressure. Even in February, when the shooting has stopped, most keepers are busy catching up surplus hens for egg-laying, mopping up troublesome pockets of rabbits and carrying out all sorts of other jobs at the end of the shooting season. When the two roles conflict, it is inevitably the deer management which suffers, and that is no more than a statement of relative priorities. I therefore urge caution when estates are considering doubling up keepering and deer management. It can work, particularly when there is a small cull, and when the roe buck programme in particular takes place when the keeper is less busy. But to achieve a heavy cull, consistently, year after year, let alone to achieve low levels of woodland damage, is simply asking too much of the individual in the vast majority of circumstances. Better by far, if a keeper likes to do some deer work, to get a good stalker to run the deer programme and allow the keeper to assist, just as other helpers assist the keeper with the game programme. In that way everybody is fully aware of the priorities, and clear about their respective responsibilities.

Setting targets for female culling

This is one of the most essential requirements of deer management in managed woodlands. My first step if I were taking on a new area of deer management would be to find out the following:

- Are damage levels too high at present?
- If so, is this damage to trees or agricultural crops or both?
- What sort of damage is taking place (see Chapter 3)?
- What are the owner's deer and woodland management objectives?
- What does the owner expect of the deer manager?

Sometimes you do not get complete answers to these questions. Often the owner or manager simply has not thought about them in sufficient depth. However, it does establish a starting point. I invariably record these early impressions and I find that not only does it help with my initial reports but it also provides a baseline against which I can measure achievements or failures as time goes by. It is rather like taking photographs – they mean much more later than they do at the time, and memory is fallible.

I form my early impressions as I walk the ground with my binoculars – no rifle at this stage – in order to get to know its boundaries, its safety features, its public rights of way and other relevant details. I look for evidence of deer damage at this stage, as well as for signs of the deer themselves. Under typical southern conditions, unless I was pretty certain that deer were being wrongly blamed for damage, I would recommend a high winter cull to start with. The size would be little more than a figure plucked from the air, with little to back it other than previous experience. There really is nothing else to go on. You need a definite starting point, and you need to set out the all-important baseline against which to work.

Assuming that the owner wanted to reduce woodland damage, or perhaps get his woodlands back into management after a period of neglect, I would normally set ambitious initial objectives, which would assume a male/female cull ratio of around 1:2. In other words I would be planning, in this first year, to shoot two female deer for every male. This plan can easily be amended the following year, or even later the same year, as more experience is gained, but it does define the starting point. If the owner's objectives were not woodland management ones I would still be advocating a male/female cull of at least 1:1.5, albeit as part of a lower overall target. There are several reasons for this, the most important being that although births are fairly evenly distributed between males and females, more males will be lost to most populations as a result of dispersion. Females seem to be much more closely tied to their home range from birth. You can see from the table what has happened in Forest Enterprise (South and West England) since the importance of increasing the female cull was widely recognised, and targets were set and achieved across this very large area of the country.

That has been the culmination of a great deal of work by staff at various levels, and represents an excellent result in my opinion. Doubtless the situation will be kept under annual review, and adjusted if experience shows a need, but I would expect that a similar cull ratio could be planned for many years or decades, with only the size of the overall cull being amended if this proves necessary.

In the early days of a deer management plan I would use local information as my basic data to help set the first year's cull. Because any figures for deer seen are likely to be much lower than the actual population I would usually plan to shoot a high percentage of the perceived population at the outset. Under normal lowland conditions it is unlikely that you will reduce the population to critical levels, even if you are good enough to achieve the figure which you have set yourself. If you do, by any chance, reduce the population to a point which you consider to be too low, a reduction in the culling level will very soon allow it to build up again. In my view it is very difficult to overcull most lowland deer

Deer Cull Returns 1995/6
Forest Enterprise S&W(E)

Ratio: Female to Male

Roe	S&W(E)	1.26
Fallow	S&W(E)	1.98
Sika	S&W(E)	1.96
Red	S&W(E)	2.32
Muntjac	S&W(E)	1.16
All	S&W(E)	1.64

populations by using ethical methods of control, although it is very easy to finish up with unbalanced populations.

When Alan and I started one deer management programme in 1982, the population was estimated at around sixty roe. We shot thirty-nine in the first year, and nobody could see any difference. We took nearly as many in the second year, and still nobody could see any difference. In fact it was towards the end of the third year of heavy culling that we started to see signs of a decline in population, and towards the end of the fourth year we reduced the cull accordingly. Of the total deer shot or known to have died during the first ten years of the management programme, we had taken 25 per cent part-way through the second year, and 50 per cent part-way through the fourth year. Over ten years we took on average one deer each year from every 29 acres (12 hectares) of land, and the annual cull on the estate ranged from nine to thirty-nine. That is just one example of roe management on a typical lowland estate, but our experience may help others to arrive at initial figures to guide the start of a management system. The important thing is to be prepared to update and amend your plans as you gain more detailed knowledge of your area. If damage levels stay unacceptably high you are not reducing the population far enough.

Summing all of this up I would suggest that it is often wise to set initial female culling targets higher than you feel comfortable with. It will stretch you and give you something to aim at, and it can always be reduced with experience. I have invariably found that if you think of a population estimate which seems reasonable and then double it, this will usually give an acceptable starting point from which to build your culling plans. You will also be seen to be taking action, and that gives landowners and managers confidence in you. Never be afraid to modify plans either upward or downward in the light of knowledge. That is not showing weakness or incompetence, it is the exact reverse – it is showing sensitivity, adaptability and a willingness to learn and improve. Keeping good records are a great help in this process, and I shall discuss it in more detail in Chapter 7.

Selecting females for culling

When asked how he selected which deer to cull many years ago, Bill Hendy replied with a wicked glint in his eye, 'If it's safe and in season and the bugger stands there long enough, I selects 'un.' That, of course, is not quite what I am advocating, but for the female cull it is not far from the truth. My own priorities, always assuming the absolute and overriding need for safe shooting, are as follows:

- Take old, infirm, crippled or unhealthy deer at every opportunity.
- Take any female which presents an opportunity for a safe shot and use a mature/juvenile ratio of around 1:1.5.
- Do not shoot the lead female among herd deer unless you want to break up the group in which case make a point of shooting her.
- If you want to shoot a female and her offspring, shoot the adult first and then wait.

Often the youngsters will return. If they do not they are almost certainly old enough to survive independently.

- Take old deer in preference to middle-aged and young ones. (Since younger beasts are easier to stalk, you will get plenty of these anyway.)

Culling seasons (England and Wales)

The open season for culling female deer (red, roe, fallow and sika) as set out in the Deer Act 1963 was well thought out and has stood the test of time. By 1 November most juveniles, although still dependent on their mothers, will stand a good chance of survival if the mother is shot. At the other end of the season it was not felt to be acceptable to subject heavily pregnant females to undue distress, and it was upsetting for stalkers to have to gralloch heavily pregnant females. The open season for female culling therefore ends on the last day of February. Muntjac and Chinese water deer still have no statutory close season, and may be legally shot at any time.

For quite a few years now, however, many stalkers have been advocating shortening the open season for male deer (1 August to 31 March for red, fallow and sika, and 1 April to 30 October for roe), and also to extend the open season for females to the end of March. I have considerably sympathy with both points. Because male deer are easier to shoot than females, and because the open seasons are longer, few stalkers have a problem with their male cull. But the occasional stalkers who have rifle certificates, who often simply want to shoot a few deer as a hobby or for a friendly farmer, tend to shoot more males because they are more obvious and easier to stalk, and also yield a bigger (thus potentially more valuable) carcase. The result is that in some areas more bucks and stags are being shot than the populations will stand. This tends to be a local phenomenon, however, rather than a countrywide problem. Nevertheless, I would guess that a reduction of, say, a month at each end of the season would have little effect on achieving sound culling plans by experienced stalkers, whilst at the same time helping reduce the 'opportunist' shooting of males.

As far as the females are concerned I have never really found a problem with orphaned youngsters on my areas, and so I think that 1 November is probably the optimum time to open the female culling season, although there would be an equally good argument in my view for opening it on, say, 15 November to add an even greater margin of security against the possibility of orphaning young deer whose mothers are killed. At the other end of the season I could see clear logic for extending it. There is no humanitarian argument in my view for not doing so, because the correct placement of a high-velocity expanding rifle bullet reduces suffering to an absolute minimum, regardless of how pregnant the female is. At the end of March most female deer are still only around 60 per cent through their pregnancy, and although the foetuses are well developed this is no more distressing (at least to me) than dealing with a road casualty or a female shot at the end of February. It would also help many stalkers get the required female cull, which would be very good for long-term woodland survival as well as for maintaining high-quality conservation sites. However, I do not see either of these changes as a major priority, more as something which I hope will be covered when there is a need for new or updated deer legislation.

Stalking on foot, using highseats and moving deer

I love stalking on foot. It is always interesting, you never know what is around the next corner and you are moving around. However I have little doubt that highseats are probably the most effective aid to shooting deer in lowland conditions. Alan and I used to have a highseat which, if it is not the highest in Dorset, must be very near to it. On a clear day its visibility is about 75 miles, with Glastonbury Tor visible to the north and the Needles on the Isle of Wight to the south. As Alan said when we put it up, 'How much further do you want to shoot?' We hardly ever used it, however, because it is cold, bitterly cold. The only time it has any shelter – and that is minimal – is when the wind is from the south-south west. From every other direction the wind goes right through you. Half an hour was quite long enough to be on it in winter and one and a half hours in summer. However, we picked up deer from it that we could not approach using any other method, and as shooting on this convex hilltop at ground level was very awkward at best, the safety margin was substantially increased when shooting from an elevated platform.

This seat was extreme – most are less climatically challenged, and the advantages of shooting at unalerted deer from above are well documented. I see highseats as extremely effective aids to deer management, but hope that there will always be opportunities for stalking on foot as well.

Moving deer, particularly during winter, is another effective aid to good management, and must be distinguished from driving them which is quite the opposite. Ideally, when moving deer I like three or possibly four reliable riflemen, though Alan and I often move small woods with just the two of us. The skill is to guess where the deer will go and place a rifle near that spot. The mover walks quietly through the wood, with his dog close at hand, perhaps tapping a stick. The idea is to allow the deer to hear him so that they get up, identify the oncoming human and move quietly away, either walking or gently trotting. The essence of the operation is not to scare them unduly. If the forward rifle stands quietly, or uses a temporary seat (which would have to be put out beforehand), he should with luck get a shot at an unalerted deer, and may sometimes collect two or three in a single move. We tend to use this technique only when we are either experiencing difficulties in a particular wood or when we are behind with the winter cull, but there is no reason why others need accept this self-imposed limitation. Properly used it is a good, effective technique.

Venison handling

The market value of venison has hardly risen during the last fifteen years. This does not help the deer manager who is trying to manage deer for woodland objectives, because it makes the economic climate even tougher, but sometimes this does actually deter the 'cowboy' element as it makes life more difficult for them as well. At the end of the day the deer manager has to take things as they come and make the best of it; but it would be very good news if venison became a prized and popular meat, and that would, in turn, affect deer management in a positive way.

Low prices, however, mean that proper carcase handling in order to bring a well-prepared product to the market place is more vital than ever. This means being able to recognise any signs which may indicate that a shot deer is unhealthy, as well as being able to turn it into a marketable product. I do not propose to go into detail here, since adequate training is available, but I will just make a few points for the benefit of those stalkers who do not have access to a purpose-built deer larder.

All shot deer should be eviscerated quickly – all body contents, from the windpipe to the anal canal should be separated from the body. In my opinion this should preferably be done within two hours of death, but if this is not possible then the carcase should be field dressed or gralloched. This involves removing the stomach, intestines, bladder and genital tracts, as well as the anus. This can be done quite simply in the field, given a little practice.

Alan and I carry a complete kit which includes carcase labels, a lightweight hoist, a set of scales and some gambrels, as well as a container of clean water and a

All shot deer should be eviscerated quickly. (RM)

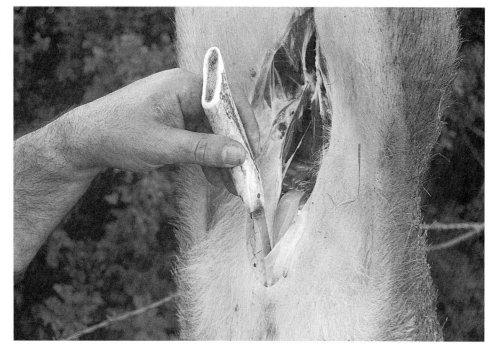

hand basin, some disposable rubber gloves, paper towels and soap. We can do everything necessary on site, and the prepared carcase can then be delivered to the game dealer ready for storage in the cold store. We can also clean ourselves up at the end of the process.

If you can get access to a cold store this is a real benefit, and means that carcases can be stored for a few days until a load has been assembled, and then taken to the dealer or collected in bulk. Not only does this make life a lot easier, especially if you live some distance from a game dealer, but it reduces the cost of transportation.

The important thing is to be as clean and tidy as possible, and we finish the job by having a leak-proof tray (in our case of fibreglass) in the vehicle, so that the carcases do not leak on to upholstery and other equipment.

It is a pity that wild venison does not have a bigger market in Britain. Whether it is because it was so easy to export it to the Continent until the late 1980s that nobody really bothered to open up the UK market, or because the modern British housewife has been conditioned not to deal with any food which is not freeze dried and wrapped in shrink wrap I do not know. I do know that it is a tasty, nutritious and largely additive free meat.

Once the carcase has been dealt with the offal must be disposed of. This rather unpleasant subject is usually neglected when discussing deer management. However, as public pressure on the countryside continues to increase, and awareness of issues of public hygiene grows, it is a subject which will assume greater prominence as each year passes.

In the past, much of this unwanted material was disposed of by burying it. But in the light, sandy soils in my area this led to problems, since badgers and foxes would dig up the contents very quickly, and it was not uncommon for the remains to be found by a roving dog, which often returned, proudly to its master bearing its find. The Forestry Commission therefore decided, some years ago, to provide specially constructed offal pits. There is no doubt that these deal with the problem very effectively, but there is a cost attached. At its simplest, an offal pit is a cylinder of fibreglass, concrete or similar material which is sunk into the ground and has a secure lid. The offal is dumped in the pit, together with a quantity of water, and rots down through bacterial action. The siting of the pits is important, in particular so as not to pollute watercourses or supplies. Consent is therefore normally needed from the water authorities (now the Environment Agency).

However, many farms and estates may have offal pits, and I strongly recommend using them. I am sure that as time goes by more and more stalkers will have to face the problem of offal disposal and public hygiene, and make provision for it, especially when shooting large numbers of deer.

Dogs for deer management

It would be difficult to discuss the deer manager's winter tasks without looking at one of his most important, but often most neglected, aids – his dog. A BASC stalking survey in 1997 found that only around a quarter of stalkers use a dog to recover shot deer. This is disappointing, particularly in light of current concerns about deer welfare and the different methods of killing them.

Most dogs can be trained to work deer and there are one or two specialists (such as Guy Wallace, who is based in mid-Wales) who will train a deer dog to a very high standard for you. I train my own, and certainly Teal, the labrador I mentioned earlier, now sadly departed, was as good as any I have ever seen. Alan's black labrador, Kestrel (sadly departed whilst the book was in preparation) was also no slouch, and although we are both ardent spaniel men for general (not deer) shooting we have gradually reached the conclusion that labradors take some beating for deer work, although many GSP, Weimaraner, Bavarian bloodhound, spaniel, flatcoat, munsterlander, Jack Russell and Yorkshire terrier owners will have different views. It does not matter a jot what breed you use, if it does the job you want it to. I would have backed Teal during his lifetime with any dog that I have ever seen working with deer, and he certainly saved us many hours of searching in heavy cover over the years.

The essential attributes for a deer dog are a good nose, a quiet and equitable temperament, and a willingness to be with you and not doing very much for long periods. Despite what I have said above, this rules out most spaniels in my view. I have owned several, including my present dog, the dreaded black and white Merlin, and all would find deer quite adequately, but after that they caused problems. After

Dogs for deer. Teal was as good as any I have seen and saved us many hours of searching in heavy cover. (RM)

Merlin would find deer quite well, but then move on to something which he found more interesting. (RM)

realising that the deer was dead and furthermore was too big to carry, they would all leave it and go on to something which they saw as more exciting. In heavy cover that is no use. Labradors love just being with their owners, regardless of what they are doing, and they often ask little more of life. Their temperament is ideal for stalking, in my view, and they are quite content to stay at heel and simply enjoy being out. Teal knew his job well and seemed to understand exactly what was required of him. He would not only find the beast but also take me to it, and that is a priceless attribute for a stalker's dog.

I train my dogs by progressing steadily through the basics and, when they prove reliable, by taking them out with me. I used to let Teal find many of the deer I had shot, although I knew perfectly well where most of them were, as it developed his skills and kept him up to the mark. I shall do the same with my current puppy as she develops. Stalking is also very good at steadying a dog: walking to heel for long periods, not moving when a shot is fired, working to command, all reinforce good gundog training. Furthermore Teal located many live deer for me which I had not seen, by 'snorting' at me as he walked to heel. Another attribute was his ability to stay under a highseat without being tethered for as long as I wanted to stay in the seat. I vividly recall one occasion when a roe buck approached from behind, to within about 5 yards before barking and retreating. Teal remained motionless and finally looked up at me as if to say, 'You could have shot him you know; I wouldn't have minded.'

6.
FINANCIAL ASPECTS

I am very grateful for the help and understanding shown by Oliver Lucas, who was my Forest District Manager for many years when we worked for the Forestry Commission (later Forest Enterprise) at Wareham, in the preparation of this chapter. Although I have invariably kept meticulous figures and collected a lot of data, like many essentially outdoor people I am not particularly skilled when it comes to interpreting them. In order to interpret figures relating to deer management which take into account the complex factors involved while encouraging real management improvements requires a level of statistical understanding which was certainly beyond my capabilities. Oliver worked away at this aspect until finally we developed a financial management system which, in my view, made a significant contribution to the deer management activities of Forest Enterprise in Dorset. It is possible that adopting a similar approach may be of use to large estates or landowning companies as well as to professional deer managers. And the basic approach to financial control can be adapted to a wide range of needs. The spreadsheet designed to fulfil this need is shown in Chapter 7.

It is precisely because of the wide range of different circumstances under which deer stalkers operate that it is very hard to put together a picture of typical deer management scenarios or to identify typical costs with any degree of confidence. All that I am able to do, therefore, is to outline a progressive approach which recognises and identifies the range of income and costs which can be associated with various options, so that, by using this approach, you can adapt any figures to suit your needs. The actual figures used in my examples are not important – it is the overall approach of considering the effects on both income and costs of each course of action, and how those actions may affect the figures, which is the key. In the current climate many deer practitioners who recognise the need to change and who want to do so, are simply forced to adopt survival tactics to maintain their own interests in this particular market place, and so the downward cycle of inappropriate deer management perpetuates itself.

In the end these things usually come down to money. I have been extremely fortunate in having dealt, in the main, with landowners who have trusted my judgement and account keeping, and that is welcome and refreshing. But I remember many years ago, when I was the accredited stalker for a deer management society, there was a good deal of suspicion amongst many of the farmers and landowners in the area in which the society was operating, and this is really the problem which so many deer management groups face. Although they are very necessary, and are arguably needed more at present than ever before, they must operate across lands which are in different ownerships. If there is any weakness in their interpretation of the rules or in their record keeping or accounting then some owners, and indeed some stalkers, will always seek to exploit them, and many good deer men are more gifted with the rifle than with the politics of their situation.

If a national overview of deer is necessary – and I would argue that one is badly needed – and if new moves such as the Deer Initiative are to succeed, then ways will have to be found to give landowners real confidence that their trust is not being misplaced – and that will usually come down to the calibre and integrity of the people who will run such groups, and even more importantly the reputation and integrity of the stalkers involved.

With no national overview of deer management, landowners and managers simply do what they think is best or follow their own strategy, which may have been developed many years before, and which may now have been overtaken by the passage of time or events. Whilst independent, local management has much to commend it, particularly when managing roe, which have a smaller range, I still believe that a national overview would be helpful in providing much-needed perspective. The development of a sustainable attitude towards deer, which sees them as part of a living but fragile countryside and recognises the most appropriate ways of managing them across a wide range of different circumstances, is also needed. This overview needs to be addressed at national and regional levels, whilst specific deer management for any particular locality will always be best done at local level. It is the national overview which appears to be lacking, and some deer managers would probably argue for a body to provide it, such as a Game and Fisheries Department, for example. This would also link neatly into a national carcase tagging system, which could also have a beneficial effect upon marketing venison, as well as making the disposal of poached deer carcases more difficult.

For herd deer (red, fallow and sika), which have extensive and seasonal ranges, balanced long-term management is simply not possible without co-operation by most, if not all, of the landowners across whose lands the deer roam. As more information becomes available about the actual extent of deer ranges, it may become possible to target such owners more precisely, but that is, as yet, some way into the future. It may be that the ranges, even of herd deer, may be substantially smaller than has hitherto been thought, and if that is so then co-operation may be needed from fewer owners in future in order to manage any particular herd, which would simplify matters somewhat, although it will still be vital.

It is a credit to the resilience of deer populations that so far they seem to survive – even thrive on – fragmented, sometimes unbalanced and potentially disastrous management. Each year, evidence is provided by some stalkers that male populations, in particular, are being decimated in some areas, and without a national overview that trend seems likely to continue, and could eventually have far-reaching consequences.

Whilst many people attempt to make a living from deer stalking, and therefore the costs of their deer stalking activities as well as their potential for income generation are presumably extremely important to them, others work on an 'expenses only' basis, providing a service for landowners whilst getting their 'hobby' at low cost. Others are prepared to pay for their stalking. It is therefore impossible to describe a typical stalking set-up – there is no such thing. But we must try and determine the baselines from which different deer enterprises operate if we are to understand why there is a critical need for change. In the final analysis such change can only be driven by the landowners who have control, and if they are to be persuaded that it is necessary then the full financial implications need to be considered. And before we can consider them we need to know what they are.

There are three elements which have a substantial bearing upon the viability of any commercial venture: whether it is possible, realistic and sustainable. It may help our assessment if we look at some existing deer management practices to see how they fit these criteria, and whether there is common ground upon which to build different solutions. I hope that this chapter will encourage landowners and managers to take a wide-ranging rather than a narrow view when they look at deer management on their estates. I believe that although the approach I am advocating involves taking some risks, the potential benefits and long-term sustainability will usually far outweigh them, whilst the risks themselves are, in my view justifiable. In the end this approach will be better for the people who actually manage the deer, better for the estates which need deer management, and better (though undeniably different) for the stalking clients who bring much-needed revenue into the system.

Taking management decisions about deer

To begin with, we need to understand who may be affected by any decisions which are made about deer management on any particular estate. They will include some, if not all, of the following:

- the landowner or the owner of the rights to take deer on the land
- the farm or estate manager
- the land agent
- any tenant farmers or other tenants (for example conservation organisations leasing land or managing it under permission)
- the stalking tenant
- the forestry or woodland manager
- the gamekeeper

In an ideal world, all the parties affected by the decision-making process would be involved in and 'own' that process – at least in part. But in my experience, this rarely happens; to the extent that key decisions are shared or discussed beforehand in a meaningful way. The result can often be friction between the deer stalker, the tenant farmer(s) and the farm manager or the gamekeeper, and in the final analysis it will be the quality and sustainability of deer management and woodland management that will be adversely affected.

The market for deer stalking

Let us look at what typically happens when stalking rights are leased. Generally this follows the classic 'market forces' approach, which often means that somebody, usually the land agent, seeks the highest rent for the stalking that the market is thought to be able to bear. Presumably rentals are based on experience of what past lessees have been prepared to pay – I have never been able to identify a more objective approach, or one which has any basis in financial sustainability.

Many stalkers do themselves no favours, because they have been prepared to pay what appear to be unsustainable rents in order to secure stalking rights. I can understand such an approach from recreational hunters, to whom this might simply be no more than an affordable sum rather than a viable proposition from a business point of view, but I know of many instances where so-called professional deer stalkers have offered outrageous sums in order to secure stalking rights, and some have even advertised in the sporting press. It is clear to the informed observer that the sums do not add up, so presumably the aim in such cases is either to secure a monopoly in a given area, complete a portfolio of recreational hunting opportunities or with an underlying intention to operate around the margins of any agreements.

> **Very little research has been done on lowland stalking values, and the rent you are expected to pay is often simply the highest figure the landowner or his agent has heard is being charged for stalking. Only after several seasons does the penny drop, with landowners realising that the higher the rent, the poorer the job of deer management is likely to be.**
>
> **Dominic Griffith, *Shooting Times*, 27 March 1997**

I can quote two recent cases which highlight this phenomenon. The first involved a close friend of mine who was carrying out some low-key deer management for a Dorset landowner. The land in question was marginally over 50 acres (20 hectares) in size, and was bounded on three sides by a large forestry plantation. My friend was shooting five or six deer each year, and the annual plan for this small cull was discussed each year with the ranger who operated in the forest next door. Each year a plan was agreed which was considered to meet the needs of all parties. Everybody was happy with this arrangement until a professional stalker offered £1,500 to rent the stalking for a year. The landowner was quite naturally, tempted, and wanted to know whether his existing stalker could match that rental figure which equated to £27.70 per acre per year (£68.40 per hectare). To put this offer into perspective, the value of venison from a typical carcase from that land (say a sika hind weighing 55 pounds (22.6 kg) dressed weight) would be around £50 at typical 1996 market values. It would therefore be necessary to shoot one deer on every 1.8 acres (0.72 hectares) of ground each year, simply in order to recoup the rent. I know the ground well, because I was responsible for the deer management in the neighbouring forest for many years, and it was very unusual for the total receipts from deer from the neighbouring 300 acres (121 hectares) of woodland to exceed this suggested rent for 50 acres (20 hectares) of land. In my view it would be impossible to show a business return by using any normally accepted ethical methods of deer management, if that land were to be leased at the rent offered.

So how can one explain the fact that somebody would be prepared to offer such a sum? There are three possibilities. First, the person concerned may simply have wanted the area at any cost, with money no object. Secondly, he may simply have been greedy, in which case market forces would force a reappraisal sooner or later. If this happened the owner could easily be left in the lurch, having got rid of someone who was providing a good and reliable service, and being left with a tenant who could not sustain the chosen management system. The final explanation is rather more sinister. The tenant may have already worked out where he could overexploit. He would have had to shoot any deer which stepped onto the land, regardless of sex, age or quality – and he would certainly have to 'short change' his clients as well, probably by double or treble booking. Even then it would be difficult to make the system sustainable, and no consideration whatever was being given to the interests of the neighbours.

In actual fact the landowner in question did not take up the offer, possibly because he realised that it was simply commercially untenable; but the offer caused substantial friction with the existing stalker, who sensibly offered to pull out if the owner decided to take up the offer.

The second case involved me personally. Another 'professional' stalker recently approached a landowner for whom I had been carrying out deer management for many years. Without making any enquiries about whether any deer management was currently in operation, he made an offer to rent the stalking, and promised 'substantial income' for the owner. All of this was done with no knowledge of the land – unless it had been visited without permission. The landowner, who is a relatively young man, remarked that if there was enough in it to enable him to retire he might be interested; otherwise he was quite contented with his existing arrangements. How such an offer could be made before the stalker had even seen the land or had any idea of the deer population, I fail to understand. I have stalked on that land on an 'expenses only' basis for many years, and the landowners have had regular reports detailing all the work that has been done and exactly what has happened to the money from venison sales. They have never wished to have fee-paying clients or to maximise income from deer; they simply wanted to see the deer properly managed and the woodlands improved, and the system we set up to do this has proved to be sustainable and, in terms of woodland viability, very successful. However, had I not built up such close relationship, I could easily have lost that area on account of an offer which simply did not add up.

Is there a place for ethics?

When I first started stalking it used to be common practice for stalkers to refuse to take on any ground where somebody else was operating unless the landowner was dissatisfied with the current stalker and was prepared to terminate his agreement. I have certainly turned down offers of stalking in similar circumstances, and I know of many others who have done similarly. Nowadays market forces, coupled with the demand for recreational stalking, seems to have opened up the deer world to a range of competition which has the capacity to do enormous harm to sustainable deer management. Nobody minds fair competition, but some sort of moral underpinning seems to me to be vital. Perhaps it is time to reappraise the moral code which should support the legal framework by which stalkers are bound; nowadays ethical considerations appear to count for nothing. What this does, so often, is to undermine good deer management which, because of its very nature, is time-consuming and detailed, and to replace it with get-rich-quick schemes, which usually die a natural death when the available resource has been overexploited.

The following story from my own experience underlines the need for an ethical approach. Whilst working for the Forestry Commission it was my practice to spend a few moments chatting to our stalking clients whenever I encountered them at the forest office or in the deer larder, so that I could find out how they viewed the service my team was providing. I did not make it formal or obvious, but if I bumped into a client I would invariably have a brief chat. One such client was down from London for a week's stalking with Eric Masters. If my memory serves me correctly, he had shot three very ordinary roe bucks – no notable trophies at all. I was surprised when I asked him whether he had enjoyed his week with us; I was expecting him to be slightly frustrated at not having found a better buck, despite the fact that he had booked to take run-of-the-mill beasts. But his reply was, 'I have had a wonderful week – one of the highlights of my life. I have booked again for the autumn already.' As I chatted to him it became clear that what he had valued was the total experience of stalking with Eric: tapping into his extensive knowledge of deer and other wildlife, and seeing skilled fieldcraft at first hand. I have often heard this view repeated since, with other Forestry Commission and private stalkers who provided a complete stalking experience. I was nevertheless rather puzzled, because although I had absolutely no doubt about Eric's skill, I failed to see what was so special about a week's stalking which seemed to me no better than average. So I asked him where he had stalked previously. He quoted a well-known professional stalker, and said that he had stalked with him for seven years. And in his view, there was no comparison. 'For a long time I enjoyed it because I didn't know any better. At each visit I would be taken to a highseat, sat in it, told what was shootable, and collected three hours later. In those seven years I never had an accompanied stalk, nor did I ever succeed in shooting a deer. Finally I decided to look for something different, and finished up here. There is absolutely no comparison. What I am looking for, and what I have found here, is a total stalking experience, of which shooting a deer is only one element.'

In the final analysis the individual must decide what represents value for money. But I can begin to understand how stalking can attract such high rents, if clients can be relieved of their money so easily and with such little return. Once this client realised that he was paying for a high-quality service, whilst being provided with an absolute basic one, he looked elsewhere. His experience also reflected badly upon the estate, even though he had purchased his stalking excursions from the stalking tenant and not the estate itself. In his mind he connected his bad experience with the estate, and its reputation took a substantial knock.

It would be easy to write this story off as an isolated case, but my conversations with many other stalking clients over the years have convinced me that similar experiences are commonplace. The problem is that, because of the very nature of stalking, the evidence of unethical behaviour is usually anecdotal, and therefore, if we are to draw conclusions from it, we must be satisfied that the observer is to be trusted. That is why the experiences quoted in this book are picked out from my own experiences or those of my close and trusted colleagues.

Instances such as these damage the reputation of deer stalking hugely, and a bad impression of the host estate is another, if rather more subtle, consequence. I have spoken to clients who have said that they will never stalk on certain estates again, even though in some instances the stalking tenant who gave them a bad experience no longer operates there. This may seem unfair, since the estate is simply suffering the consequences of the actions of an undesirable tenant. But at the end of the day it is the estate owner or agent who sets the rent levels, and it is artificially high rents which either lead to or exacerbate such situations. Of course, even in the best-run operations there will always be the odd occasion when things do not go according to plan, or when there is simply a run of back luck, but that is very different from plain bad practice.

These situations arise in my view because we treat deer as a sporting resource rather than as a part of estate management. When sport drives the system, the system is inevitably sport orientated. We need estate management to drive the system, with the possibility if it is considered desirable by the managers responsible, of tapping into increased income from sport stalking. In that way the needs of woodlands and habitats are given precedence, and deer management is structured to meet that need. Recreational hunting may then be used as a means of generating additional revenue where it is considered that this is compatible with the more important management objectives. Only if matters are approached in that order are they likely to change for the better.

In recent years I have begun to hear of professional stalkers who lost deer management agreements on certain estates because somebody had offered a higher rent, but who have been asked to come back several years later, when the owner or agent finds that the high rental system is unsustainable, and that the estate has been left with major problems which it did not have before. The good professional, who knows what the real costs and possibilities are, and who does not set out to overexploit clients, landowners or deer, is a real asset to any estate, and is capable of providing an efficient and sustainable service which will meet most needs. If landowners, land agents or farm or forest managers try to see their stalkers as providers of a much-needed and individually tuned service, they will begin to see the real value of their work. If they look at deer management differently and set objectives which actually meet their wider needs, they will find that the stalker will usually respond. All that is needed is a different approach to the situation, judging success by rather different parameters than simply the level of income received from stalking rents.

Whilst I would not argue with the right of any individual or organisation to offer whatever it thinks appropriate for any marketable commodity, at the end of the day there is a finite income which can be generated, and if the price is too high then something has to suffer. In the case of deer I would argue that in the long term it is all too often the sustainability of woodland management which suffers when deer management objectives are short-term and unbalanced.

Leasing deer stalking – is it good value for landlords?

Getting the maximum possible income for stalking rent is not the same as getting the best financial performance, although in straightforward terms of marketing there is much to commend this approach, since it requires minimum input and achieves maximum immediate income. In terms of sustainability, however, it is frequently disastrous. By sustainability in this context I mean the organisation and running of a deer management system which meets the objectives set by the landowner, provides an acceptable level of return for the deer manager, and can continue to deliver such returns over many years.

Deer management is no different from anything else: there is a price to be paid when the 'easy income' route is chosen. As we have seen, the price which is often paid for this narrow, short-term approach has been either overexploitation of the deer resource for sport or the implementation of deer management options which are incompatible with woodland management. I shall demonstrate that the costs incurred through poorly targeted deer management can easily outweigh the short-term financial gains from stalking rents.

I will start by considering straightforward rents for deer stalking, for it is the level of rent which determines the flexibility of the deer management system which may subsequently be used. Often the stalking rent is seen as income for the estate which has been generated by letting the deer stalking. There is a simple and obvious connection between the two factors. But whilst many people try to anticipate the possibility of deer damage, the probable implications of poor deer management in respect of increased woodland management costs rarely form part of an overall assessment. The connection between poorly targeted deer management and increased woodland management costs is less obvious, and therefore often overlooked.

A professional stalker who leases stalking rights has to make his operations pay their way. In this he is often a victim of circumstances. If the rent required is so high that balanced and targeted deer management is impossible to sustain financially, then short-term measures have to be adopted to meet the needs of the moment. I know a number of deer managers who would like to do things very differently, but are not able to because this system binds them. Others who are more determined, or luckier, insist on operating a system which they find ethically and financially tenable, but frequently complain of being undercut by competitors with lower or 'more flexible' standards. It is often woodland management which suffers from all of this, yet it is possible to adopt an alternative approach which can target deer management much more effectively.

Let us look at an imaginary lowland estate which rents its stalking on the open market. Note that the figures used are for illustration only, and whilst they may represent broadly typical costs, they should not be interpreted as anything other than general examples applicable at the time of writing.

I shall make the following assumptions:

- The estate comprises 2,000 acres (810 hectares).
- The rent for the stalking lease equates to £1.00 per acre (£0.404 per hectare) per year.
- The estate has both fallow and roe deer. Fallow pass through regularly, often in reasonable numbers, whilst the population of roe is typically high and resident.
- The estate contains 500 acres (202 hectares) of woodland, which is run on semi-commercial lines. It has an annual restocking programme of 10 acres (4 hectares).
- The estate suffers substantial deer damage to unprotected trees and also to farm crops in most years, and there is constant friction between the forestry department and the deer stalker(s).
- The stalking rights are sold at market rent, and the stalking tenant is given no targets for culling or deer management by the owner or agent.

Based on these assumptions, the immediate income to the estate as a direct result of letting the stalking in this way is £2,000 per year. At first glance, this seems remarkably healthy. Substantial income has been achieved with very few associated costs – just the construction of a lease. But when we begin to look at the situation in greater depth we begin to see that there may be subsequent costs which can easily wipe out this benefit.

This estate protects its young trees and shrubs with tree shelters, or for larger areas with deer fences. It needs to provide such protection both to safeguard its investment and also because failure to achieve satisfactory levels of establishment could jeopardise the planting grants made by the Forestry Authority. As far as farm crops are concerned, the estate simply tolerates any damage, but tree planting without grant aid, particularly of broadleaved species, is financially marginal, and the vast majority of planting schemes are therefore grant aided with government funding. There is therefore a close and financially driven link between woodland management and grant aid in many instances, although there may be many different reasons why landowners choose to manage their woodlands. Since the commercial viability of most small woodlands is marginal, the provision of grant aid is an essential component of their long-term survival. When grant-aided tree planting becomes threatened by unacceptable levels of deer damage, therefore, the relationship between deer and woodland survival is put under severe strain.

Before the advent of tree shelters, which started to appear during the late 1970s, the only viable way of protecting young trees from deer damage was to deer fence them. But tree shelters are now in common use, and they have additional advantages over deer fencing in that they also protect against hares and rabbits and also provide some growth enhancement to the trees. The primary purpose of providing them, however, is to protect against deer and it is fair to point out that both tree shelters and deer fencing are expensive. Whilst costs vary considerably from place to place, depending upon factors such as the exact specification required, the size, accessibility and ground conditions of the area being planted and the experience and skill of the contractor involved, the following is a fair guide to the costs involved.

Providing a single 1.5-metre tree shelter, with its associated stake and fixings will cost in the order of £2.00, and broadleaved trees (the sort most commonly protected by this method) are planted at a minimum density (in order to attract planting grant) of 445 per acre (1,100 per hectare). Providing shelters on a planting area of 1 acre (0.404 hectares) would therefore cost something like £890 (or £2,200 per hectare). The typical cost of providing deer fencing in the lowlands will be in the region of £4–7 per running metre, so that to fence this same acre of ground (assuming a need to provide at least 280 yards (256 metres) of fence) will cost anything from £1,020 to £1,790. (As a rule-of-thumb guide it can often be more cost-effective to use shelters to protect areas which are less than about 1 acre (0.404 hectares) in size, and to deer fence larger areas, but this may vary. In order to protect the annual restocking programme in our example, therefore, we need to spend at least £890.00 per acre – £8,900 for the whole 10-acre area – and this expenditure can be attributed, for the most part to protection against deer.

The Low Bid

It is unwise to pay too much but it is worse to pay too little. When you pay too much you lose a little money – that is all. When you pay too little you sometimes lose everything because the thing which you bought was incapable of doing the things it was bought to do.

The common law of business balance prohibits paying a little and getting a lot – it cannot be done. If you deal with the lowest bidder it is as well to add something for the risk you run.

And if you do that you will have enough to pay for something better.

There is hardly anything in the world that some man cannot make a little worse and sell a little cheaper, and the people who consider price only are this man's lawful prey.

John Ruskin

The next step is to investigate whether there are any practical ways of reducing these costs, and to do this we have to put the deer management under scrutiny. In my opinion it is possible to control most lowland deer populations so that satisfactory tree establishment is possible without the need for protection in the form of tree shelters or fencing. This was standard practice during my service in large commercial forests with the Forestry Commisison, and I have also achieved viable tree survival of coppice and natural regeneration in very small-scale broadleaved woodlands, so I know that it is achievable, though not always necessarily applicable. At the time of writing I am less sure whether I shall be able to achieve similar results where young broadleaved trees are *planted* (as opposed to regenerating from seed), in small areas (less than 0.5 hectares (1.3 acres)), as deer do seem to be attracted to planted trees rather more. However, over the next few years I shall make every effort to find out.

If one accepts this view, it follows that any costs incurred as a result of protecting woodland habitats against deer has become necessary as a direct result of selecting an alternative deer management option. These costs are essentially avoidable, and should therefore be set against any income from the letting of deer stalking rights if a balanced view of the financial implications of the chosen deer management options is to be obtained.

I must make it clear that I am not recommending any particular option for deer management – that must always be the prerogative of the landowner or manager, and should be decided on the basis of what is best for the particular estate. What I am saying is that only when the real financial implications of various options are understood can the consequences of following them be assessed against objective criteria. If, for example, the sporting aspect of deer stalking is judged as being of overriding importance to a particular estate, then that will obviously influence the choice in favour of that particular option. But at least by following the approach suggested here, and by adapting the figures to individual cases, the financial implications will be identified, and that, in itself, will lead to better-informed deer management.

Returning to our analysis of deer-related income and expenditure from our lowland estate, we see the following picture:

- Income from stalking is £2,000.00
- Expenditure on protection is £8,900.00
- The net loss is therefore £6,900.00

Even if we assume that only 50 per cent of this loss is attributable to deer (and that is a very optimistic assumption), we can see that in this example there has been no overall income from deer stalking at all – there has actually been a loss, and quite a substantial one. The perceived income from letting stalking rights does not now seem as attractive in the face of the costs which have been generated as a direct result of selecting that particular option.

Let us now look at what might happen if a different approach were selected. Let us assume that a deer manager is engaged, who will be expected to operate with a different objective – simply to manage the deer so as to minimise damage to forest and farm crops and woodland vegetation – and that he will be expected to set and update culling levels in order to meet this objective. Since he is seen as providing a service to the estate, no rent is charged. He is not paid directly, but the proceeds from venison are shared on a previously agreed basis between the landlord and the deer manager. (This is not a typical scenario yet, but it may have a great deal to commend it, and I do have personal experience of how it works in practice.)

Let us assume that this approach leads to a reduction in the need for tree protection of 80 per cent as compared with the previous system. This allows for the provision of some protection for troublesome areas where deer damage seems to persist no matter how carefully controlled the population. Let us also assume that the annual cull needs to be 40 roe and 20 fallow in order to achieve these objectives. (The exact levels are not important, they can be fine tuned. It is developing an effective approach which is important.) Let us also make the following further assumptions:

- An average fallow carcase is worth £60.00 (65 pounds at £0.90).
- 20 carcases are therefore worth £1,200.00.
- An average roe carcase is worth £45.00 (30 pounds at £1.50).
- 40 carcases are therefore worth £1,800.00

The income from the cull programme outlined above, through sales of venison, is therefore likely to be £3,000.00. A 50 per cent share of this would be £1,500.00.

Our management equation now looks like this:

- Income from venison is £1,500.00
- Expenditure on protection against deer is £1,780.00
- The net direct loss is £280.00

The saving from the reduced protection costs is £7,120.00, so it could be argued that a gain has been made of £6,840.00, which is this saving less the overall loss resulting from implementation of the programme. But whichever way you choose to look at it, the operation has turned a loss of £6,900 into a loss of £280 – and we have not yet considered other ways of increasing income. And such figures are achievable and the system may be sustainable, given the right stalker. It certainly would be in the early years following its introduction, although I would expect some fall-off as the population is brought under tighter control.

Now we can consider how we can generate further income and make the system profitable without reducing the quality of the deer management, and this brings us back to recreational hunters. But it must be made clear that fee-paying recreational hunters must be accommodated within the defined management system. They must not be allowed to dictate the objectives of that system nor should they be allowed to influence management decisions in any way. Those decisions should be taken jointly by the estate and the deer managers, and decided on the basis of what is judged appropriate for the estate at a given point in time.

As I have said, the figures I have used here are simply examples, and no more than that. It is the approach that underlies them that is important. Use that approach; modify it to suit your own circumstances, and then construct your own set of figures to suit your needs.

Deer management is rarely straightforward and all I can do is to demonstrate the benefits to be gained from taking all relevant factors into consideration and analysing the total picture before taking key decisions. Analyse the costs as well as the benefits of any particular course of action, and select the option which best suits your needs. And be prepared to update and amend figures as you gather more information.

I believe that landowners with deer problems have a lot to gain from devising deer management systems which suit their identified long-term needs, and then in organising matters so that the objectives which have been set out can be achieved year after year. However, at the end of the day, if a landowner, agent or forester is prepared to accept what I would describe as undue deer damage, or feels that the sporting aspect is so important to the estate that the damage levels are acceptable and that the cost of protection is justified, at least the decision will have been made in the knowledge that alternative strategies exist.

One view of what stalking may actually be worth to a professional hunting guide was put forward recently by Dominic Griffith, in an article in *Shooting Times*. He considered a rental of £0.50 per acre per year could be sustainable. My view is that it depends what your objectives are. The system he is suggesting still appears to be driven by sport rather than by woodland management, but his contention suggests that current rent levels are too high even for that objective. And as we have seen from my example, the income from letting stalking is often counterbalanced by subsequent expenditure on tree protection. Whilst the exact figures are largely irrelevant, we saw that by implementing a different deer management regime the loss could be substantially reduced, with the added advantage of a sustainable deer management system. We should not try to draw too many conclusions from figures which are largely hypothetical, but the one clear point is that many stalking rents are simply too high to allow sustainability.

There is one further point to make, and that concerns one's expectations. If you decide to change your deer management system, do not assume that simply because you have made the right changes, things will instantly be better. The situation should certainly improve, but the improvement may take a while. If it has taken twenty or thirty years for a deer population to become unacceptably large or badly unbalanced as a result of poor management, it will take at least three or four years, and possibly longer, to get everything back under proper control. This should be built into both your expectations and your costings. Only at the point where such control is established will the true savings become apparent.

Stalking rents and the professional deer manager

I now want to look at the financial demands placed on the professional deer manager as a result of the 'market forces' approach to stalking rents. I start from the assumption that the first requirement is to make a profit from the operation, and that this profit needs to be sufficient to provide an acceptable income in relation to the actual time spent doing the job. I will use as an example again, the 2,000-acre lowland estate, with its annual demand for £2,000 in stalking rent, and I will assume that venison is sold for the same price as in that example.

The stalking tenant who took this on would need to shoot forty-four roe or thirty-three fallow each year simply in order to pay the rent, before any further expenditure is taken into account, and before he has begun earning an income. Let us assume he makes forty-four visits in order to shoot enough deer to pay the rent, averaging three hours per visit, travelling 25 miles each way, and requires a wage of £7.00 per hour. Typical costs involved would be as follows:

Travelling 50 miles at 25p × 44 visits	£550.00
Wages. 44 visits × 3 hours × £7.00	£924.00
Sundries. Ammunition, highseats, office etc.	£100.00
Total	£1,574.00

In order to recoup these costs, after having paid the rent he would need to shoot a further twenty-six fallow or thirty-five roe, which would, of course, add a further set of costs, which would generate a need to shoot yet more deer. This would provide a bare minimum wage, and the cycle is never-ending because he has to shoot more and more simply to stay level. So what happens is that he is forced to sub-lease or take fee-paying clients in order to make ends meet. There is simply no other way.

And what, you may ask, is wrong with that? What is wrong is that such a system is driven by the crushing need to use fee-paying recreational hunters in order to make it work. The economics are so fragile that everything is driven by the need to make the system pay. I have come across instances where the stalking tenant has sub-let to more than one syndicate of recreational hunters, all of whom have been led to believe that they have purchased exclusive rights. They then get very upset when they find out that they have been misled. Some cases like this have finished up in court; in others the hunter has simply been cheated. None of this does deer stalking any good, and the stalkers most at blame are those who have allowed their greed to override their commercial common sense. In the rush to make the operation pay, it is no wonder that good deer management goes out of the window.

Let me take that argument one stage further and suggest that when any management system is driven by its clients, those clients' desires override everything simply because if they do not get what they want, they can take their custom elsewhere. Where deer stalking is the commodity being marketed, most clients want to see plenty of deer, and to be given opportunities to take ever better trophies. There are of course stalking clients who are genuinely interested in wider deer management principles, but they generally prefer to follow their own desires rather than the needs of the woodland manager or the estate. In fairness, when they have paid handsomely for the privilege, it is perfectly natural for them to do so. None of this leads to a system of deer management which is aimed primarily at meeting the long term needs of the landowner. It exists to satisfy the perceived need of the fee paying client and may, coincidentally, meet short-term financial considerations of the landowner, which may be a different thing entirely.

In organisations such as the Forestry Commission and some of the larger forestry and woodland management organisations the approach is often different. They know the likely costs of poor deer management. There is much more emphasis upon driving costs down, as well as achieving adequate levels of protection, and recreational hunting will usually be seen as distinctly subservient to this need. In Forest Enterprise in recent years various initiatives to reduce the cost of deer management have been tried with varying degrees of success. The stalking in some remote areas has been block let, and in other areas contractors have been brought in to carry out deer control, and the advantages and disadvantages of each system are still being analysed, so much has yet to be learned.

An alternative approach

A different approach to deer management which would be transparently fair to both landowner and deer manager and which would be worth considering, would be to contract it out on the basis of previously agreed shares. One way of doing this might be to agree that total income from venison sales will be shared on an agreed basis, whilst the profit from using fee-paying clients will be shared equally once the deer manager has taken out his legitimate operating expenses. If it then proves to be a bad year, both the owner and the deer manager share the misery, whilst if the year is better than expected both can share the extra rewards. The owner still has the final sanction – he can simply get rid of the deer manager if he wishes. An annual review should always be built into such a system, and this should look at actual achievements. In that way realistic figures are used and updated, and risks and rewards are fairly shared. Of equal importance, such a system should prove both effective and sustainable in practice, whilst also providing a highly flexible response to changing conditions. The landowner, woodland manager, deer manager and any fee-paying, stalking guests are, effectively, stakeholders in a shared system of risk and reward, rather than locked into a competitive and potentially confrontational system, which in the long term may serve nobody very well.

7.
RECORD KEEPING TO AID
DEER MANAGEMENT

Keeping records for the future

A s you manage the deer on your area, working to your predetermined plan and learning about the animals, what information can you gather which can help you to improve your management, and how do you record it?

Keeping good records is vital. Not only do they provide clear evidence of what is happening and what you are achieving, but they also build up into a database for the future, from which you can learn a great deal. Of course, they also highlight weaknesses or potential weaknesses in your system, and some people feel uncomfortable with this, but there is no need to do so as long as you are prepared to take action to deal with weaknesses, and good records often point directly to areas where improvements may be necessary.

There are many possible recording systems, but I will describe the records I keep and how these interrelate to provide me with the management information I need. This is the system which I have used in private deer work but, with their kind permission I will also touch on the Forest Enterprise financial control system as it applies to deer management, and as it was pioneered and is currently used in the South and West England region. In this way I can show you how both large and small programmes are recorded, and whilst it is not my intention to discuss specific financial arrangements I will also display four models of computerised record keeping which have assisted my deer management over the years.

I keep a small notebook in which I enter every deer known to have died on the areas in which I am interested. The information I record is as follows:

- code number of the deer killed, species, sex and age group
- date, time, weather and location
- stalkers out that day
- the stalker who shot the deer or the person who found a dead (unshot) deer
- calibre of rifle, bullet weight, range of shot, reaction to shot
- dead weight of carcase (if convenient), butcher's weight (always)
- any undue damage to the carcase
- whether pregnant and number and sex of foetuses
- whether stalked, shot from a highseat or moved to rifle
- aids used – stick, bipod etc.
- shot position – standing, kneeling, prone etc.
- remarks and other interesting details

From these details I can complete my stalking diary, my venison sales record, my stalkers' expenses, my annual reports and anything else I need as part of my deer management system – including, eventually, much of the background for this book. And it is not very much trouble – it takes two or three minutes at the most basic level for each beast. I have, in recent years been adding these records to my computer database – with mixed success, but that is definitely the way forward. Computers can analyse data very effectively, and we have much to learn from past records. I now run spreadsheets for venison sales as well as databases with diary details, and having set these up, the machine does the sums for me.

Perhaps I should explain how I use some of these records. The code number gives each deer a unique identification so that I can tell which estate it was shot on, and where the carcase was sold or disposed of, as well as a cross reference to all records relating to that animal. Each carcase is labelled, so that the game dealer also has a reference. For some estates where there may be more than two stalkers operating, the code includes a letter which identifies the stalker. The age is recorded as female adult, female juvenile, male adult or male juvenile.

As far as weight is concerned I use dead weight to mean the weight of the animal as it fell. Where it is necessary to field dress it I cannot always record this weight. Butcher's weight is the weight of the prepared carcase which has been fully eviscerated, with the head and lower limbs removed but with the skin intact. This takes no account of carcase damage, which is assessed separately with the game dealer and an allowance made if appropriate. I know of stalkers who record weights before and after gralloching, and in many different ways, but my system provides me with everything I need, and is consistent. This information goes straight on to my venison sales spreadsheet, and from there into annual reports and records of payments to owners, as well as being used to distribute stalkers' expenses.

The information on pregnancy is useful, and gives clear indications of the reproductive potential of any population, and also how this may be affected by other factors such as culling pressure, as well as the proportion of males to females conceived, and therefore potentially recruited into the population.

The other details recorded give information about various aspects of deer management, from the proportion of deer shot from highseats to the times of day which appear to be most successful for culling, all of which is peripheral rather than vital, but I see it as worth recording.

Using computers to aid deer management

Love them or hate them computers are here to stay. I see a computer in much the same way that I see a rifle, a pair of binoculars, a camera or any other item of equipment. It is a good servant but a very bad master. I am in favour of anything which helps me to do any aspect of my job better or more easily, but I am equally against having to adapt my working system to the needs of a machine which is really a glorified adding machine. I therefore have a love-hate relationship with my computer, but gradually it is beginning to serve me more than I pander to it. Computers do provide deer managers with a very useful tool to help keep good records, as well as having the capacity to analyse past data so that it can be used to improve deer management, and I expect that the new generation of stalkers will take to using them much as my generation adopted telescopic sights.

I adopt the following approach. From my field notebook the information which relates to stalking goes onto individual cards on a computer database (an example of which may be seen in figure 1. By using the database approach to replace my old manuscript records, I hope to be able to analyse all of this information further, with the aim once again of improving my deer management. The problem does not lie in analysing the data, but getting all of my past records onto the system. Information which relates to deer habits and ecology is also recorded on database, on similar cards, so that, one day, it may be analysed more carefully.

Speadsheets have many potential uses in deer management. My colleagues and I made much use of a spreadsheet designed by Oliver Lucas the Forest Enterprise District Manager at Wareham, to analyse costs and returns from the Dorset deer management programme each year (see figure 2). Introducing the spreadsheet led

Figure 1. Stalking records, database format.

Code No		Date	Time		Species		Sex/age
TW 306		**6.8.97**	**0730**		**Roe**		**Male adult**

Stalker	Stalkout	Shootpos		Where hit	Range		Reaction
AL	**RM/AL**	**Standing/bipod**		**Neck**	**75m**		**Fell inst**

Pregnant	Stal/Hst	Rifle/ammo	Weight dead		Weight Butcher's	
N/a	**Stalked**	**308 × 150**	**N/A**		**34lbs (15.5 kgs)**	

Antlers/coat
Summer coat. 7″ × 5 pts. R = 3pts, L = 2pts (lacks 1st pt). Good pearls, unusual head.

Weather
SE1/2. Intermittent heavy showers with torrential rain starting at 0815

Location   **Ridgeway. OS 5830. On fenceline dividing the long fields**

Remarks
Alan found this poor but unusual buck on the hilltop in the wheat crop. The buck responded to the call, and Alan was able to get a safe shot looking along one of the tramlines. The buck dropped on the spot, but we got drenched an hour later when collecting it in the pouring rain.

Figure 2. Forest Enterprise deer management spreadsheet.

DEER MANAGEMENT – ANALYSIS OF PERFORMANCE AND DAMAGE BY FOREST YEAR

Notes: Net income figures appear as minus
B = Budget Target
A = Actual Performance

	LINE	SOURCE	92/93B	92/93A	93/94B	93/94A	94/95B	94/95A	95/96B	95/96A	TOTAL TO DATE 92/3 to 95/6
FC CULL PROG											
No deer culled	2	SW40/S105									
Expenditure	3	FC32									
Income	4	FC32									
Net Expenditure	5	Line3–4									
Forest Area (hectares)	6	FC32									
DAY PERMIT PROG											
No deer culled	7	SW40/S105									
Expenditure	8	FC32									
Income	9	FC32									
Net Expenditure	10	Line8–9									
Forest Area (hectares)	11	FC32									
TOTAL FOREST DISTRICT PROG											
No deer culled	12	Lines 2 + 7									
Expenditure	12	FC32									
Income	14	FC32									
Net Expenditure	15	Line13–14									
Forest Area (hectares)	16	FC32									
SUMMARY											
FC CULL PROG											
Net cost per deer £	Lines 5/2										
Net cost per ha £	Lines 5/6										
DAY PERMIT PROG											
Net cost per deer £	Lines 10/7										
Net cost per ha £	Lines 10/11										
TOTAL PROG											
Net cost per deer £	Lines 15/12										
Net cost per ha £	Lines 15/16										

Notes for readers: FC 32 is a regularly produced printout of budget performance
SW40 and S105 are FC deer management records
xx/yy means xx divided by yy.
FC Cull Programme means all deer culled by Forestry Commission rangers
Day Permit Programme means all deer culled by recreational hunters under FC control
Total Programme is an analysis of the total deer management programme including both elements described above

to significant management improvements, as the deer management team could see each year exactly what was happening, and the manager in charge of the programme (which at the time happened to be me) could decide whether adjustments were necessary, and if so where they needed to be made. This spreadsheet also showed how much income was coming in from client stalking, as well as from venison sales, as well as areas where expenditure was taking place; and the system therefore allowed ready comparison with budget targets. However, the value of any such system depends almost entirely on the accuracy of the information being collected, and the allocation of income and expenditure to the correct accounts, and such an approach is most likely to be of use where large programmes are being controlled.

It would be straightforward to refine this system even further to include levels of deer damage, although these would need to be expressed in financial terms, thus quantifying the scale of the loss. It would therefore be possible to design spreadsheets for individual estates which would accept annual targets for deer management, in respect both of income from various sources and of necessary expenditure, and which would allow comparisons of different options and results.

In my own system, all information relating to venison sales is transferred onto a spreadsheet for each estate (an example can be seen in figure 3). Once set up, the spreadsheet calculates the value of each carcase, the stalker's expenses and the balance to the owner, and provides the financial statement for my annual reports. It also gives instant up-to-date feedback whenever required or as each new entry is added. Every carcase is cross referenced to its code number and the game dealer's delivery and payment slips.

Finally this information is summarised for each estate on an annual report (a copy of the format I used is shown in figure 4). These reports provide a permanent record of deer management over many years, and their value increases as more information is gathered.

I would always advise against using figures slavishly, particularly where a complex task such as deer management is concerned, because other factors might be involved. Nevertheless they do highlight various aspects of management which are inescapable. Both successes and failures are identified, thus enabling managers to investigate further if required, should improvements seem to be called for. Figures on their own do not, of course, remove the need for a thorough understanding of the operation. They represent yet one more tool which, if properly used, can lead to improvements in management, and it needs little imagination to see how computers can be used as powerful tools to aid deer management, as well as assisting managers in accurate target setting and performance monitoring. That way represents the route towards improving deer management through the application of modern technology.

Figure 3. Venison sale spreadsheet.

Venison Sales   Spreadsheet

PERIOD FROM   1.4.97 to 31.3.98

Estate: Anyold Estate

Code No	Date	Location	Shot By	Buck Wt/lbs	Doe Wt/lbs	Both Wt/kgs	Dmge Y/N	Wt for Sale lbs	Price per/lb £	Value £	Expns x%	Baln Ownr £	Owner 1 £	Owner 2 £	Sold To	Date Paid	Remarks
					0.0			0.0	£0.00	£0.00	£0.00	£0.00					
								0.0		£0.00	£0.00	£0.00					
								0.0		£0.00	£0.00	£0.00					
								0.0		£0.00	£0.00	£0.00					
								0.0		£0.00	£0.00	£0.00					
								0.0		£0.00	£0.00	£0.00					
								0.0		£0.00	£0.00	£0.00					
								0.0		£0.00	£0.00	£0.00					
								0.0		£0.00	£0.00	£0.00					
								0.0		£0.00	£0.00	£0.00					
								0.0		£0.00	£0.00	£0.00					
								0.0		£0.00	£0.00	£0.00					
								0.0		£0.00	£0.00	£0.00					
								0.0		£0.00	£0.00	£0.00					
								0.0		£0.00	£0.00	£0.00					
								0.0		£0.00	£0.00	£0.00					
								0.0		£0.00	£0.00	£0.00					
								0.0		£0.00	£0.00	£0.00					
								0.0		£0.00	£0.00	£0.00					
								0.0		£0.00	£0.00	£0.00					
								0.0		£0.00	£0.00	£0.00					
								0.0		£0.00	£0.00	£0.00					
								0.0		£0.00	£0.00	£0.00					
								0.0		£0.00	£0.00	£0.00					
								0.0		£0.00	£0.00	£0.00					
								0.0		£0.00	£0.00	£0.00					
								0.0		£0.00	£0.00	£0.00					
								0.0		£0.00	£0.00	£0.00					
TOTALS FOR YEAR				0.0	0.0	0.0	0	0.0	£0.00	£0.00	£0.00	£0.00	£0.00	£0.00			

Notes:
1. Baln = balance. Dmge = damage.
2. Owner 1 and Owner 2 are where there are more than one owner involved.
3. Value = Wt for sale multiplied by price per lb.
4. Expenses = agreed percentage to cover stalker's expenses/share of income
5. Baln owner = value minus expenses.

Figure 4. Deer management, annual report.

**Anyold Estate Deer Management
Annual Report**

To: Period from:
                                                        1 April 1997 to 31 March 1998

Dear,

DEER MANAGEMENT REPORT

SECTIONS
Cull Plan and Results
Venison Sales
Statement of Accounts
Next period
Items of Interest

Signature and Date

CONCLUSION

This book has drawn together a wide range of topics under the general heading of deer management, so in conclusion it seems appropriate to summarise the main points we have discussed:

- Wild deer in Britain have no natural predators. Population control can therefore only be exercised by man.
- Deer managers need to be aware of the vital differences between *stalking* and *deer management*, and to recognise which option is best under different circumstances.
- They also need to be aware that if sustainable woodland management at an acceptable cost is an important management objective, the deer management system should be designed to meet the woodland management objectives rather than the other way around.
- Where sustainable woodland management is important, deer numbers will normally need to be kept artificially low.
- Working out how many deer to cull should be approached first by looking at deer pressure on the habitat, and secondly by relating this to known past deaths in the population, amending future culling plans in the light of this assessment.
- The key to regulating the size of deer populations lies in culling sufficient females to achieve the stated management objectives.
- The quality of a deer population is strongly influenced by the selective culling of males.
- When assessing the value of any deer control activities it is important to look at the costs which are incurred as well as the income which is generated.
- It is important to be able to attribute crop damage to the correct cause.
- Defining appropriate management objectives is vital if deer control is to successful. Communicating those objectives to the deer cullers is equally important, as is revising them from time to time in order to meet changing needs.
- Formal attempts to count wild deer populations often result in inaccurate results, and can be costly as well as wasteful of time and effort. Gathering information which has been collected whilst stalking throughout the year and using this instead costs nothing and gives equally good results.
- It is usually only possible to age deer under field conditions by putting them into the loose categories of young (juvenile), middle-aged and old.
- Muntjac present an unusual and different set of management problems.
- It is possible to accommodate recreational hunting within effective deer management for woodlands, but only if it is regarded as a subsidiary activity instead of the controlling influence.
- When building recreational hunting into a deer management system, it is wise to ensure that deer management is driven by the woodland needs, and that clients are then accommodated within the required deer management system. This ensures correctly targeted priorities.
- Having said this, always give fee-paying hunters value for money through the quality of the experience you provide.
- Cull poor males, regardless of the cull plan. Unless numbers of males are excessive, leave good males to breed. Adjust the final cull by deciding whether or not to shoot mediocre males.

- Do not attempt to cull females selectively, at least until populations are firmly under control. Take any shot which is safe and within your capabilities, unless the selected female obviously has a dependent offspring.
- Choose your equipment to match your requirements. It is usually wiser to economise on a rifle than on a telescopic sight, providing that it is sound and accurate.

Shooting deer, for whatever reason, is a serious business. In my opinion, nobody should set out with the intention of killing a deer without a basic understanding of deer ecology and habits, without the ability to take a safe shot and place it into the killing area, and without the knowledge to turn the resulting carcase into a useable product. This shows respect for the quarry and the competence to carry out the task in hand. A stalker who has become proficient at this basic level and then graduates to managing deer begins a much steeper learning curve and accepts a challenge which will test his commitment and enthusiasm as well as teaching him a lot about himself.

If your deer management role lies in ensuring that deer and their habitats are properly managed within the areas where you have responsibilities, I hope this book will have given you some pointers to help you set and achieve realistic priorities and objectives. Whatever your role in working with deer I hope that I have provided you with some of the answers that you have been looking for. There is much still to learn, but if I have encouraged a wider and more critical approach towards deer management, and if this leads to more carefully targeted work, then my efforts will have been well worth while.

INDEX